abundant *life*
DAY BOOK

abundant *life*
DAY BOOK

365 BLESSINGS
TO BEGIN YOUR DAY

NANCY GUTHRIE

TYNDALE

Tyndale House Publishers, Inc.
Carol Stream, Illinois

Visit Tyndale online at www.tyndale.com.

Visit Nancy Guthrie's website at www.nancyguthrie.com.

TYNDALE and Tyndale's quill logo are registered trademarks of Tyndale House Publishers, Inc.

Abundant Life Day Book: 365 Blessings to Begin Your Day

Copyright © 2011 by Nancy Guthrie. All rights reserved.

Cover pattern copyright © nicoolay/iStockphoto. All rights reserved.

Butterfly illustration copyright © Neubau Welt. All rights reserved.

Wrap photograph of sunset copyright © Jelena Veskovic/iStockphoto. All rights reserved.

Designed by Al Navata

Unless otherwise indicated, all Scripture quotations are taken from the *Holy Bible*, New Living Translation, copyright © 1996, 2004, 2007 by Tyndale House Foundation. Used by permission of Tyndale House Publishers, Inc., Carol Stream, Illinois 60188. All rights reserved.

Scripture quotations marked ESV are taken from *The Holy Bible*, English Standard Version® (ESV®), copyright © 2001 by Crossway, a publishing ministry of Good News Publishers. Used by permission. All rights reserved.

Scripture quotations marked NIV are taken from the Holy Bible, *New International Version*,® *NIV.*® Copyright © 1973, 1978, 1984, 2010 by Biblica, Inc.™ Used by permission of Zondervan. All rights reserved worldwide. www.zondervan.com.

ISBN 978-1-4143-4818-6

Printed in China

17 16 15 14 13 12
 7   6   5   4   3   2

*Blessing is the pronouncing of God's favor.
It includes the gifts that God gives as the
evidence of His love and favor, but blessing is
more than what God gives. It is the bond of
favor that joins God's people with Him.*

Dr. Edmund Clowney,
The Unfolding Mystery

INTRODUCTION

Have you ever wondered why we say "God bless you" to people when they sneeze? There was a time when sneezing was a symptom of the deathly plague. And because getting the plague was considered a sign of God's displeasure, saying, "God bless you" when someone sneezed was offering a prayer that the person would receive the blessing of God—ongoing life—rather than dying from the plague. To be blessed is to have life—abundant, overflowing life.

In the best-known blessing from the Bible, we read that the Lord instructed Moses to tell Aaron and his sons to bless the people of Israel with this special blessing:

> *May the LORD bless you*
> *   and protect you.*
> *May the LORD smile on you*
> *   and be gracious to you.*
> *May the LORD show you his favor*
> *   and give you his peace.* (Numbers 6:24-26)

God wanted his people to enjoy the assurance of his intention to bless them. From this special blessing we learn that to be blessed is to see the smile of God over our lives rather than to live under his frown. It is to experience his ongoing grace rather than expect his condemnation. It is to enjoy God's favor rather than endure his rejection. It is to be at peace with him rather than being his enemy.

Experiencing God's blessing is not merely getting good things from God. The essence of blessing is God himself. When we begin to see how much God has given to us in Christ, and how much he is worth, we realize that all of the things we were hoping to get from God—good health, loving relationships, protection from harm, material provision—are only temporary, tangible reminders of all we have in Christ. As blessed people we can say along with the psalmist:

> *I desire you more than anything on earth.*
> *My health may fail, and my spirit may grow weak,*
> * but God remains the strength of my heart;*
> * he is mine forever.* (Psalm 73:25-26)

As we begin this journey together over the next year, there are two important things you must know. First, while I've taken great liberty in writing these blessings as if they are God speaking to you, the only aspect of each day's blessing that has the authority of God is the Word of God quoted at the top of each page. Writing as if it is God who is speaking is only a device employed for the purpose of helping you hear him speak his blessing personally to you. My hope is that it will serve to make the Scripture come alive and become even more precious to you. I have sought to be faithful to God's Word in expounding on it and applying it using this literary device, and have done so with a sense of holy fear, prayerfully seeking to be one "who correctly explains the word of truth" (2 Timothy 2:15).

Second, you need to know that the Bible makes it clear that while God offers his goodness to all who will embrace Christ by faith, he does not force his blessing on those who do not desire him. But if you want him, he will freely give himself to you. You do not have to earn God's blessing (in fact, you can't earn it!). You do not have to deserve God's blessing (in fact, no one deserves it!). You cannot twist God's arm or wrestle his blessing from his reluctant grasp using the right technique or the right prayer. This life with God is not about what he wants you to do for him, but what he has done for you through Christ.

If you have lingered away from God, fearing what he will demand of you, unsure of all it will mean for you, you need not stay away any longer. If you have settled for trying to be a good person or a spiritual person, you can become a completely new person. You can turn to Christ and take hold of him by faith. Tell him that you want to belong to him, to know him and be known by him, to be changed by him. He "is being patient for your sake. He does not want anyone to be destroyed, but wants everyone to repent" (2 Peter 3:9) Then you'll be able to celebrate that he "has enabled you to share in the inheritance that belongs to his people, who live in the light" (Colossians 1:12).

That is what this book is about—the blessing and inheritance that belong to God's people. I invite you to celebrate that blessing and revel in that inheritance. I invite you to drench your soul in this steady stream of God's blessing given to you freely and fully in Christ. I hope that you'll open this book day after day along with God's Word, and that you'll open your life to all that God has given to us in Christ, confident that because "he did not spare even his own Son but gave him up for us all, [he will] also give us everything else" (Romans 8:32).

Nancy Guthrie

I Am Making You into a New Person

Anyone who belongs to Christ has become a new person. The old life is gone; a new life has begun! And all of this is a gift from God.   2 Corinthians 5:17-18

In your old life you lived for yourself—for what brought you temporary pleasure, for what made sense in your worldly way of thinking and had value in your worldly way of measuring worth. I love you far too much to let you linger in that old life. That life is gone for good. The old you is gone for good. I've made you into a completely new creation—fresh and new on the inside—blessing you with a fresh perspective about what really matters and a youthful vigor for pursuing me.

This newness is no self-willed fix-yourself-up, become-a-better-you self-improvement project. Your newness is not an effort I required of you but a gift from me, a work of my Spirit from start to finish.

I know I am new, and yet I find myself so easily embracing old habits, old grudges, old patterns of thinking. I'm turning toward you today, Lord, so that I can walk in this newness of life in the words I speak, the thoughts I think, the pleasures I enjoy . . .

I Have More Blessing for You Than You Know

From his abundance we have all received one gracious blessing after another. John 1:16

When you ask me to bless your plans, I wonder if you really know what you are asking for. To be blessed is to experience and know more of me. To ask me to bless your life and your efforts is to invite me into the center of them. That is the essence of blessing, the joy of it. Oh, how I long to bless you! I want to share from my abundance one gracious blessing after another.

To be blessed is to be deeply content in me. It is to make your home so securely in me that nothing can shake you. You can be blessed in the midst of a miserable situation, because being blessed doesn't mean you have no trouble or struggle or sorrow; it doesn't mean you always experience success and comfort. Instead, it means that in the midst of the trouble and struggle and sorrow, you find yourself deeply secure, profoundly content, and happy in me. To know me, walk with me, and share life with me—that is the essence of blessing.

I am incredibly blessed! In the hard places as well as the good times, I am finding more of you than I have experienced before . . .

I Have Said "Yes!" to You

All of God's promises have been fulfilled in Christ with a resounding "Yes!" And through Christ, our "Amen" (which means "Yes") ascends to God for his glory.   2 Corinthians 1:20

Hear me saying "Yes!" to you throughout your day. By giving Jesus to you, I am living up to every promise I have made to my people throughout the ages. Into eternity you will be blessed by my abundant fulfillment of my promises to you. I've promised you peace, and I've given you Jesus, who is your peace. I've promised you joy, and Jesus is your joy. I've promised you a life that is meaningful and worthwhile, and it is Jesus living through you that makes your life meaningful and worthwhile.

Whenever you might be tempted today to think that I am withholding anything good from you, remember that I have given you my very best in giving you Jesus. In him you have everything you truly need, and more than you even know to ask for.

God, I hear you saying "Yes!" to my every need through Jesus, and I say "Yes!" in response to whatever you ask of me today . . .

I Myself Will Bless You

May the LORD bless you and protect you. Numbers 6:24

All the goodness you desire in this life comes from me. It doesn't come from having things or enjoying pleasant circumstances, but from relationship with me. You do not have to work or manipulate to extract from me the goodness you long for and the resources you need. I give to my people freely. All I have is yours in Christ, given freely, abundantly, eternally.

To experience and enjoy my blessing, simply cling to me. Cling to me in the pleasant places of life. Cling to me in your darkest hours. Come to me early in your day and throughout your day. Remain in me when your patience is tested and your strength is gone. Rest in me when you are tempted to simmer in anger or agonize in anxiety. Whenever you are tempted to think that I have been unkind, unfair, or untrustworthy, close your eyes and hear me whispering, "I myself will bless you."

I open my hands to receive all you want to give me today.
I place my life in your hands, resting in your promise to
protect me . . .

I Am Working Out My Plans for This World

God has now revealed to us his mysterious plan regarding Christ, a plan to fulfill his own good pleasure. And this is the plan: At the right time he will bring everything together under the authority of Christ—everything in heaven and on earth.
Ephesians 1:9-10

When it seems to you that everything about this world has careened decidedly off course, you can rest easy, confident that everything is really falling right into place. Human history has never been determined by the decisions or actions of mere humans. And the future of this world and all who live in it will not be guided by mere fate. I am Lord over history and Lord over time, and I am guiding this world to its appointed destiny.

You do not need to live in fear that a dangerous dictator, a dreaded disease, or an environmental disaster is going to displace my plans for this world or for your life. Of this you can be certain: All of my plans will one day fall into place, and all of my promises will become the reality you will live in and enjoy into eternity future.

How I long for the day when I will see with my eyes what this world will be like under the authority of Christ . . .

I Will Bless Your Brokenness

Jesus took some bread and blessed it. Then he broke it in pieces and gave it to the disciples, saying, "Take this and eat it, for this is my body." Matthew 26:26

In this world, when something is broken, it is often considered useless and thrown away. But in my economy, brokenness is not cause for being cast aside. It is your brokenness that actually makes you useful and pleasing to me. The sacrifice I want is a broken spirit. Brokenness is not the automatic result of experiencing deep hurts; rather, it's a lifestyle of agreeing with me about the true condition of your heart. It is shattering your self-will so that the life of Jesus might spill out of your life. It is continually responding to conviction with humility and obedience.

It was in his broken body that Jesus accomplished the work of salvation. Jesus has shown you what it means to be broken and to be used by me in painful but beautiful ways.

Broken Savior, used by God, as I remember your body, broken for me, I begin to see my heart the way you do. I fall down in brokenness and repentance before you . . .

Walking in My Ways Brings Real Blessing

Be careful to obey all these commands I am giving you. Show love to the LORD your God by walking in his ways and holding tightly to him.   Deuteronomy 11:22

To know me, walk with me, and share life with me—this is the essence of real blessing. And the truth is, it is the hard things in your life that cause you to want to know me more intimately, walk with me more closely, and share life with me more fully. That is why, in the losses of life, you can find yourself blessed beyond your imagination or expectation. Because you have found more of me in these hard places.

When you look up from your hardship with a smile, you know you've moved from just hearing my Word to living it— putting it to the test. You're finding that giving is better than receiving, neediness is better than self-sufficiency, trust is better than worry. You've discovered that my Word is true, my joy is your strength, my promises are your hope, my presence is your comfort. This is the life of blessing you always longed for but didn't expect to find in this way.

What a blessing to walk with you and hold tightly to you both when the sun is shining and when there is only darkness. Lord, you are the real blessing in my life . . .

I Will Make You Clean

When he had cleansed us from our sins, he sat down in the place of honor at the right hand of the majestic God in heaven.
Hebrews 1:3

When the radiance of my glory shines into your life and reveals what is there, you cannot help but wonder how you will ever become clean again. It seems impossible. But I have provided what you need to get rid of the stains of your past failures—the blot of divorce, the ugliness of cruelty, the emotional debris left behind by sex outside of marriage, the filth of what you've let your eyes see, the contamination of the words that have passed your lips, the corruption of your selfish motives, the utter apathy in your heart toward me.

You do not have to get your life cleaned up before you give yourself to me. Come to me as you are, and I will take away the ugliness of your sin. Trade in your sin-stained record, your sin-plagued thoughts and motives, and even your spot-ridden righteousness for the righteousness of Christ, the purity I offer as a free gift.

Purify me, Lord. I am utterly ruined by sin, and I simply cannot clean up my act on my own. The blood of Christ is the only cleanser that will take away the stains sin has left in my life . . .

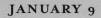

I Have Provided a Mediator

There is only one God and one Mediator who can reconcile
God and humanity—the man Christ Jesus. He gave his life to
purchase freedom for everyone. This is the message God gave to
the world at just the right time.   1 Timothy 2:5-6

I made you and I loved you, yet we were estranged because
of the destruction brought by sin. The distance between us
brought me enormous pain and brought you enormous deprivation. Something had to be done.

So I made the first move. I reached out my hand of reconciliation, my hand of undeserved friendship, by sending my
Son as a mediator. Though he was violently rejected, that did
not put an end to my reconciliation project. He made peace
possible by offering himself as propitiation. Those who have
received my Son have found themselves reconciled to me. The
relationship is restored, the blessing resumed.

My blessed Mediator, Jesus Christ, you have done it all and
given everything to bring me back into God's good graces. Only
you could make things right . . .

I Am Disciplining You for Your Good

God's discipline is always good for us, so that we might share in his holiness. No discipline is enjoyable while it is happening— it's painful! But afterward there will be a peaceful harvest of right living for those who are trained in this way.
Hebrews 12:10-11

I know you don't want to be disciplined. Too many times you've experienced punishment that was delivered out of anger, and so you recoil from the very idea. But my discipline flows out of my love, not my anger. I am not mad at you and I don't want to hurt you. However, I am willing for you to hurt a little so that you can share in my holiness.

My discipline is never too harsh or inappropriate. I always know what the right discipline is for you. And while the hardship itself might not be what you would describe as good, you can be confident that because you are my child I will use it in your life for a good purpose. The grand aim of my discipline is to make you holy and happy like Jesus. If you are willing to be trained by my discipline—molded and shaped by it—you will enjoy the peace and joy that comes from knowing everything is right between you and me.

I'm submitting to your discipline, Father. I long for a growing holiness in my character, rightness in my living, and peacefulness in my countenance . . .

I Fill Your Life with Significance

My dear brothers and sisters, be strong and immovable. Always work enthusiastically for the Lord, for you know that nothing you do for the Lord is ever useless. 1 Corinthians 15:58

You long for your life to be well spent—for it to count for something that will last beyond your last breath. I do too. That is why I have called you into my Kingdom work. You can be assured that nothing you do for me, no hour or effort you invest in my cause, is misspent. You will not go to your grave having wasted your life. You will have invested it in the only thing that will last forever—my Kingdom.

So as you give yourself away to people who don't say thank-you, as you go out on a limb and face criticism, as you deny yourself to live up to your financial commitments to my Kingdom, don't think for a minute that you'll regret it. Every slice of your time, every portion of your income, every ounce of energy you give away for my cause, you will not lose, but in fact will have invested for eternity.

Your promise reminds me that as I work and give and die to myself, the day is coming when I will stand before your throne with no regrets, only a deep sense of satisfaction and significance . . .

I Will Define True Blessing for You

*The LORD had said to Abram, "Leave your native country,
your relatives, and your father's family, and go to the land that
I will show you. I will make you into a great nation. I will
bless you and make you famous, and you will be a blessing
to others."* Genesis 12:1-2

Just as I called Abraham to step out in obedience to my word,
leaving all that was familiar and comfortable to go to a place
that I had not yet shown him, so am I calling you to radical trust. This is not just a track for the superspiritual. There
is only one kind of relationship anyone has with me, and it
involves staking your life on what you cannot see—my promise of blessing.

Following Christ demands that you give up control, predictability, ease, comfort, familiarity, affordability, and auton-
omy. I offer no up-front guarantees that you'll always approve
of my plans for your life or that you'll always feel ready for
the next step I call you to take. But I do guarantee that my
blessing will more than match the longings of your heart. The
fulfillment of my promises will go beyond your own ambitions by an infinite degree.

*Instead of clinging to what is familiar, I will cling to your
promises. You have called me to follow you in a grand adventure
of faith, and I would be a fool to set any preconditions . . .*

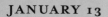

I Will Show You Ever New Displays of My Grace

So that in the coming ages he might show the immeasurable riches of his grace in kindness toward us in Christ Jesus.
Ephesians 2:7, ESV

Heaven will not be endless sameness, but will unfold in ages—one new era after another, each an ever-clearer manifestation of my infinite goodness. This is the very purpose of my salvation. I have saved you so that I might spend an eternity showing you the overflowing exuberance of my love.

Your experience of me will not come from your powers of discovery but through my power on display. The atmosphere of heaven will be wave after wave of my glories—a wave of purity that rinses away the poisons of cynicism, a wave of truth that will wipe away all of the lies you've listened to, a wave of intimacy as you see my face and feel the touch of my hand wiping away your tears, finally knowing how much you are loved and how close I will be forever. You will gasp in joyful wonder over new and startling displays of the richness of my grace.

While I am often predictable and boring, you, God, are endlessly surprising. You will hold me awestruck over the ages of eternity to come . . .

I Intend to Give You Your Heart's Desires

Take delight in the LORD, and he will give you your heart's desires. Psalm 37:4

I know that when it comes to loving me, you have always been more comfortable with the language of obedience and duty. But I'm not willing to settle for a passionless relationship with you. I want your heart. Not because I am needy, but because I know you are needy. Your deep need is not necessarily for more discipline but for more desire for me, more delight in me.

I want you to take delight in me like you savor a fine meal, like you linger in the presence of a good friend, like you celebrate the accomplishments of your child, like you look forward to a restful day of vacation. Bring me your appetites and feed on me. Dive into life with me, allowing me to envelop all of who you are. Celebrate me, listen to me, hold nothing back from me. When you do, you will find your yearnings satisfied, your desires fulfilled.

As I actively seek to delight in you, Lord, I'm finding that you are becoming my heart's fondest desire, and you are giving me more of yourself . . .

I Will Fight for You

The LORD himself will fight for you. Just stay calm.
Exodus 14:14

You are not being paranoid when you sense a powerful evil in this world that is always seeking to snuff out your faith and weaken your confidence in me. You have an enemy who is always plotting to harm you, deceive you, destroy you. But I have not left you alone to reckon with this evil. You are not even out in front leading the charge. The place for you is resting in me, hiding yourself in me. I am out front. I will fight for you.

You see, at the Cross, I defeated the enemy—sin—and broke the chains it had wrapped around your life in the form of idols and addictions. Turn to me and enjoy that victory. I have shined a light on the true nature of those things that used to look so inviting and attractive so that you can see how depleting and destructive they are. Delight yourself in me and let me give you what is most desirable.

The more clearly I see your mighty power exercised for me and not against me, and the closer I draw to you, the more I understand what your victory on the Cross means for me . . .

You Live under the Freedom of My Grace

*You also should consider yourselves to be dead to the power
of sin and alive to God through Christ Jesus. Do not let sin
control the way you live; do not give in to sinful desires. . . .
Sin is no longer your master, for you no longer live under the
requirements of the law. Instead, you live under the freedom
of God's grace.*   Romans 6:11-12, 14

There was a time when you had no power to say no to sin. It
was a way of life. But now you have been united to Christ,
and when he died, so did the old you who was a slave to sin.
And when he was raised to new life, so were you.

While you still face temptation, you are no longer a slave
to foolish impulses, fleeting pleasures, and sin's false promises.
Sin is no longer the dominating power in your life. My grace
is the life-giving power at the center of your life. I am taking
away your love of sinning, even as I have taken away your guilt
for sinning. I am giving you an appetite for holiness so that
the taste of sin will become bitter.

*Gracious Master, give me eyes to see your beauty and glory so
that in your light I will see the true ugliness of sin and say no
again and again . . .*

I Love to Give You Good Gifts

*You fathers—if your children ask for a fish, do you give them
a snake instead? Or if they ask for an egg, do you give them
a scorpion? Of course not! So if you sinful people know how
to give good gifts to your children, how much more will your
heavenly Father give the Holy Spirit to those who ask him.*
Luke 11:11-13

I am your Father and you are my child, so you can pray with a
sense of security in my love. I am much more inclined to hear
and help you than the best of human fathers. You will never
find me out of sorts, unconcerned, or unavailable.

But you should know that because I love you, I will not
always give you what you ask for. It is not mere stuff that I
want to give to you. Indeed, everything you collect in this
world you will one day be forced to let go. No, I want to give
you something far better than wealth or health or the things
that mortals love to collect. I want to give myself to you. So
ask for more of my Spirit at work in your world, in your
church, in your family, in your heart.

*Father, you give good gifts—indeed, the best gifts. And I'm
asking for more of your Holy Spirit . . .*

I Have Saved You from an Empty Life

You know that God paid a ransom to save you from the empty life you inherited from your ancestors. And the ransom he paid was not mere gold or silver. It was the precious blood of Christ, the sinless, spotless Lamb of God. 1 Peter 1:18-19

There is an empty way of life passed down from generation to generation that largely goes unquestioned. But I simply cannot let you spend the capital called your life on what is trivial, fleeting, and ultimately of no lasting impact or worth. I intend to make your life count. I have paid what is of infinite worth so that you can turn away from what is worthless and live for what is meaningful, substantial, eternal.

I'm not interested in tweaking the life most people take for granted, but in replacing it with something supernaturally significant. I don't want you to merely add Jesus to your established life, but to trade that vacuous life for one that will generate waves of impact now and into eternity.

I worship you for ransoming my empty life at the cost of your precious blood. I can no longer think of you only in terms of what you ask of me, but of what you have given for me . . .

I Am Calling You Away from Your Selfish Ways

Calling the crowd to join his disciples, he said, "If any of you wants to be my follower, you must turn from your selfish ways, take up your cross, and follow me." Mark 8:34

When I call you to take up your cross and follow me, I am calling you to die—to put self to death. To be my follower you must die to your desire for worldly respect, for an easy life, and for earthly wealth, among a thousand other deaths. And while this may sound at first like loss, it is no grim invitation into a stoic life of self-sacrifice for a noble cause. Instead, it's an invitation into joy beyond imagination. The only things I ask you to deny yourself are those things that will rob you of eternal joy.

I'm calling you to deny yourself the world's paltry, brief joys so that you may have overflowing eternal joy. I'm calling you to deny yourself hell that you may have heaven.

My bent toward pleasing and worshiping myself is so deeply ingrained in me, Lord. But these things bring only fleeting pleasures. I want to deny myself what will ultimately bring me misery so that I can embrace your eternal joys . . .

I Have Brought You into a Place of Privilege

Because of our faith, Christ has brought us into this place of undeserved privilege where we now stand, and we confidently and joyfully look forward to sharing God's glory. Romans 5:2

There are many things in life that you cannot be sure about. You cannot be sure how long your life will last or what shape it will take. But there are some things of which you can be absolutely certain, and one of them is this: you will share in my glory. You were made for this very purpose: to enjoy the riches of my glory. You will not only see my glory, you will share in it. It will not only be revealed to you but in you.

Does this promised blessing move you? Does it thrill you? Does it fill you with holy anticipation? As you fall more deeply in love with my glory, and as you nurture your longing to share in my glory, you will become impervious to the assaults this world inflicts on you. Let the certainty of my Word and my track record of keeping my promises thoroughly convince you that you are not destined for the grave, but for glory.

It is truly an undeserved privilege you have lavished on me—to live day by day confident and full of joy, knowing that your glory will one day be the reality I will share with you forever . . .

I Will Bring You Back into My Garden

The LORD God planted a garden in Eden in the east, and there he placed the man he had made. The LORD God made all sorts of trees grow up from the ground—trees that were beautiful and that produced delicious fruit. In the middle of the garden he placed the tree of life and the tree of the knowledge of good and evil. Genesis 2:8-9

Long ago I planted a garden in Eden, a place where those I created could enjoy the richness of beauty and satisfaction and, most of all, unfettered relationship with me. And ever since Adam and Eve traded the perfect blessing of the pure Garden for the painful Curse of being expelled from the Garden, I've been at work to bring you back. Christ came to put an end to the Curse, and when he comes again, the Curse will be gone for good. Then you'll be brought back to the bounty and blessing of a garden paradise where nothing will ever come between us again.

Great Giver of all that is good, how I long for the day when I will enjoy all of the goodness and bounty you've prepared for those who love you . . .

I Have Put Christ in Charge of It All

This is the plan: At the right time he will bring everything together under the authority of Christ—everything in heaven and on earth. Ephesians 1:10

When you look around and see the rise of tyranny or the decline of morality, an increase in apathy or a decrease in piety, you need not fear. This world is not spinning out of my control. I am at work bringing all things to their appointed end. I have put Jesus in charge of this world and everything in it. There is nothing he does not have authority over, nothing he does not have the right and the power to do with as he pleases.

While most people think that they are in charge of their own lives and the master of their own destiny, you know better. The day is coming when at the name of Jesus every knee will bow, in heaven and on earth and under the earth, and every tongue confess that Jesus Christ is Lord. On that day, no one will question who is in charge. The entire world will see what you have known all along—that Jesus is over all.

Jesus, I gladly recognize your authority over my work life and my leisure, over the way I spend my money and the way I live out my sexuality. You are Lord of my passions and preferences, Lord of my present and my future . . .

I Am with You Wherever You Go

This is my command—be strong and courageous! Do not be afraid or discouraged. For the LORD your God is with you wherever you go.   Joshua 1:9

Walking through life with me does not mean that there is never any struggle, or that you will never face opposition or difficulty. It means that you can encounter whatever comes without being crippled by fear or depleted by discouragement. Instead, you can know a strength and courage that comes from your settled confidence that I am with you. I am out in front of you, leading you into the abundant life I have promised to give you. I am beside you, speaking words of encouragement and instruction, pointing out potential dangers. I am in you, filling you with my power and conforming you into the image of my dear Son.

When I tell you I am with you, I do not mean I am present in a general sense, but in a personal sense. You have my attention and affection. Wherever you go, you can reach out and find me right beside you.

I do not want to go anywhere that takes me away from you. And I don't have to fear. You are with me wherever life takes me . . .

What I Require of You, I Give to You

By his divine power, God has given us everything we need for living a godly life. . . . In view of all this, make every effort to respond to God's promises.   2 Peter 1:3, 5

I never ask anything of you that I do not also provide to you. I do not expect you to attain true godliness on your own. In fact, you can't. You must have everything provided for you by me. You need to know me, and I have made myself known to you. You need to take hold of my promises, and I have held them out to you.

But while I have given you everything you need, this does not mean that you should be passive. My goodness and my promises should inspire your every effort to delve further and further into my endless grace. You must work out your salvation even as I am at work in you. Wherever you are today in your journey toward godliness, take the next step. Make every effort because I am worth it.

The mark of true salvation is divine power employed for growing godliness—an increasing love for me and walking in my ways.

I find that the more I know you and experience you day by day, the more I am changing. And it is not just the power of my will. It is divine power, provided by you, doing its work in me . . .

I Have Chosen to Bring You Close

Though we are overwhelmed by our sins, you forgive them all.
What joy for those you choose to bring near.   Psalm 65:3-4

I know that you often feel overwhelmed by your sin, and I'm glad, in part, for that. The fact that you are aware of your sin and feel the weight of it, the offense that it is toward me, the distance that it takes you from me—this is true blessing. To be cursed is to be so far away from me and so at home in sin that you do not sense sin's weight.

My blessing is not just making you aware of your sin but granting you a great forgiveness that covers all of your sin. Though your sin looms large before you, my forgiveness looms larger.

When you are discouraged by your slow progress in becoming holy, find joy in remembering that I have chosen to bring you near to me. I will not neglect you. As you linger in my holy presence I am burning away your bent toward sin, and one day you will stand before me not only forgiven, but purified and holy.

Thank you for blessing me with an awareness of my sin, and thank you for your abundant forgiveness . . .

I Will Change How You Feel

Even if we feel guilty, God is greater than our feelings.
1 John 3:20

Some might say that you feel the way you feel, and you can't really change it. But I have not saved you to leave you helpless in the area of your emotions. As my Spirit takes residence in your inner life and goes to work, he does not just cause you to act differently and think differently. He causes you to feel differently. He changes how you think about me and about your circumstances, and therefore how you feel.

How you feel flows out of what you believe—not what you think you ought to believe, but what you truly believe. Joy and peace flow out of your solid belief in my promises. Fear and fury flow out of your unbelief in my provision. So when you feel lonely, inform your feelings of the truth that I am with you and will never leave you. When you feel resentful, inform your feelings of my gracious forgiveness toward you. When you feel anxious, inform your feelings of my protective care for you.

Lord, I want you to rule over all of me—my thoughts and beliefs, my actions and reactions, and even my feelings. May my belief in you be lived out not only in how I think, but also in the way I feel . . .

I Have Given You Credit for What Christ Has Done

Abram believed the LORD, and the LORD counted him as righteous because of his faith. Genesis 15:6

You could have read about all I have promised to provide for you in Christ and discounted him, or simply disregarded him. But, instead, you have embraced him. You have heard the good news of Christ and have let me make it a part of you. You have put your full weight down on Christ, even though you can't see him with your eyes and don't fully understand all that he is and all he has accomplished. You have believed.

Because you have believed, I have blessed you by making a transfer to you. I have credited to you the righteousness of my dear Son. This is not your own goodness. It is not a wage you have earned by believing, and neither is it something that magically appeared out of nowhere; this is real righteousness. Your faith is the channel through which you have received the perfect righteousness of Another.

You alone are my righteousness, Christ. You have given to me what I could not earn or accomplish on my own. Your goodness to me and credited to me is overwhelming . . .

My Acceptance Will Change You

"Where are your accusers? Didn't even one of them condemn you?"
   "No, Lord," she said.
   And Jesus said, "Neither do I. Go and sin no more."
John 8:10-11

Don't wait for your sin to be exposed. Dig up the truth about yourself and bring the whole ugly mess into my light. I am not your accuser and I will not throw stones. Whatever anyone else may say, whatever you may say to yourself, I will not condemn you. I will save you and cleanse you.

The new life you need begins not with humiliating condemnation but with overflowing acceptance. Will you just step into the light and stay long enough, without flinching, for my acceptance to change you? I can say to you what no one else has the authority to say: Your sins are forgiven.

To be uncomfortably embarrassed by your sin as it comes under my penetrating gaze is better than to be comfortably undisturbed by hidden sin. Exposure to my light is your salvation.

I am bringing my sins, one by one, into open view, so that you can forgive me and cleanse me. I believe you came to save me, not to condemn me . . .

I Am Who I Am

God said to Moses, "I AM WHO I AM."   Exodus 3:14, NIV

I have given you, my creature, the privilege of knowing me personally and calling me by my name. In fact, it is imperative that you know who I am. My very name tells you that I am unchanging, constant, unending, always present, always God. I am the Center of everything. I am the Beginning and Ending, the Resurrection and the Life, Savior, Restorer, Builder, the Answer, Wise One, Coming One, Mighty One.

I Am all that you need now and forever. When you have questions that need answers, problems that need solutions, I Am. You find my sufficiency at the end of every desperate prayer. When you need help, when you need hope, when you need insight and understanding, I Am. When you need a fresh start, the full picture, something lasting, something real, someone you can trust, I Am. When no one is listening, when you don't know where to turn, when you can't hold on any longer, I Am.

Whenever I dwell on my feelings of being unloved, unnoticed, or insignificant, it is because I have forgotten that I know the God of the universe on a first-name basis. I'm calling on you now, I Am, knowing full well that I am not . . .

I Will Share a Secret Satisfaction with You

When you give to someone in need, don't do as the hypocrites do—blowing trumpets in the synagogues and streets to call attention to their acts of charity! I tell you the truth, they have received all the reward they will ever get. . . . Give your gifts in private, and your Father, who sees everything, will reward you.
Matthew 6:2, 4

It can be tempting to live out your life of faith and good works in a way that will earn the admiration of other people. But you should know that if you are giving and living for others' approval, you should enjoy it thoroughly, because that is all you can expect to get.

If you will reach outside of yourself to give to those in need out of a desire to please me, and if you will do it in a way that doesn't draw attention to yourself, you can be confident that I will reward you fully. As you turn away from seeking public applause and instead seek my private approval, you will enjoy the secret satisfaction of knowing that you have pleased your Father.

I am discovering the pleasure of enjoying your satisfaction with my deeds done in secret and anticipating hearing "Well done." . . .

I'm Giving You Confidence in What Is to Come

Faith is the confidence that what we hope for will actually happen; it gives us assurance about things we cannot see.
Hebrews 11:1

Living in this world, surrounded by need and sorrow and disappointment and death, continuing to believe that I am the source of plenty and joy and fulfillment and life, requires faith. It takes a radical reliance on my Word—specifically my promises about the day when the healing and wholeness I've secured for you will become the reality you see and know and enjoy.

You know that you are living by faith when, because you are confident of the joy and value of what is to come, you hold loosely to the things of this life. You are confident because you've been given tastes and glimpses of my goodness in the here and now that have given you substantial assurance of what you hope for. To live by faith is not to have confidence that I will make everything okay for you in this life, but that I will more than make up for the pain and difficulty of this life in the next.

My happiness doesn't depend on my current circumstances but on future joys. My life is worth living now because of what it will be forever . . .

I Will Be Kind to You

God is both kind and severe. He is severe toward those who disobeyed, but kind to you if you continue to trust in his kindness.   Romans 11:22

I am kind to repentant sinners. My kindness flows out of my perfection. But I am also severe with unrepentant sinners, and my severity also flows out of my perfection.

Some would rather ignore the reality that I am a God who brings judgment, preferring to think of me only as a God of love. But I don't want you to reduce me by making me into your own version of a god you can explain, a god who does what makes sense to your limited understanding. I want you to know me as I truly am, to see the full breadth of my character and interaction with those I created. I want you to see not only my tenderness but also my toughness. Revel in my salvation, but don't forget my judgment. See my welcoming friendship, but see, too, my fierceness toward those who reject me. It will serve your faith well to understand my severity because it will send you running into the arms of my kindness.

I love you for being kind, and I love you for being severe. I want the blessing of knowing you in the fullness of who you truly are . . .

I Have Set Out a Feast for You

Jesus said again, "I tell you the truth, unless you eat the flesh of the Son of Man and drink his blood, you cannot have eternal life within you." John 6:53

In today's world it is cool to embark on a spiritual search, yet it is uncool to find me. But you have not only searched for me, you have found me and partaken of me. True belief in me is feasting on Christ, which is the most profound experience of the human soul.

It's not enough to be inspired by Christ's beautiful life; you must find a feast of satisfaction in his substitutionary death. You must savor his death as your life. It is not just the example of Christ's life that you need to follow. It is Christ's death you must feast on. While his life may inspire you, only his death can liberate you.

This is the continental divide in the life of the soul, the place where so many flounder and fall away. Christ must become as much a part of you as that which you eat. There must be a daily partaking, ingesting him into your life.

Jesus, I'm hungry, and nothing in this world can fill me. I will starve without you. But at your invitation I've come. I receive your dying love for me. You are enough for me . . .

Forgiveness Will Flow out of Your Being Forgiven

If you forgive those who sin against you, your heavenly Father will forgive you. But if you refuse to forgive others, your Father will not forgive your sins.   Matthew 6:14-15

I know how much it costs to forgive—to pay the debt yourself that you are rightly owed. And I know it doesn't seem right or fair to forgive the one who does not deserve to be forgiven. I know this because it is what I've done. You see, I did not forgive your significant offense toward me because you deserved it. In fact, you haven't yet seen clearly the sin in your life that was borne by my Son. Yet still I have lavished forgiveness upon you, making it the very air you breathe.

Won't you take in a deep breath of my abundant forgiveness, allowing it to empower you to forgive the one who has hurt you so significantly? I want to bless you with that power today and with the freedom that comes when you fully forgive from the heart.

My Father, I realize I simply cannot receive your forgiveness and yet refuse to extend forgiveness to someone else. But how I need your power . . .

I'm Giving You the Joy of Genuine Faith

There is wonderful joy ahead, even though you have to endure many trials for a little while. These trials will show that your faith is genuine. 1 Peter 1:6-7

I know that you think there is no room for joy in the great sorrows of your life. You think joy and sorrow are mutually exclusive. But as you live in me, you're discovering that great sorrow actually creates the capacity for deeper joy.

What can possibly be the source of joy in the midst of great loss? The joy comes in finding out that when the rubber hits the road, the faith you have given lip service to for so long is now put into action, and it is the real deal. You get to live it out. Faith moves from being an intellectual exercise to a personal adventure.

When you choose to trust instead of fear, real faith is revealed. When you choose to accept rather than complain, forgive rather than indulge in resentment, be humble rather than prove you were right—the curtain is pulled back on your life and your faith is proved genuine.

I'm finding joy, Lord, even in the hard places of my life as I'm discovering that I'm not a hypocrite. The faith I have claimed is real, and it makes a difference in how I respond to hardship . . .

I Will Make Something from Nothing in Your Life

By faith we understand that the entire universe was formed at God's command, that what we now see did not come from anything that can be seen. Hebrews 11:3

I made everything there is—all of it. And I made it out of nothing. I simply spoke it into being, saying, "Let there be . . . ," and there was.

Because you are mine, this creative power is now working in your favor. I am not limited to the raw materials available in your life; I can make something from nothing.

So when you have a need for which there seems to be no resource, remember that you belong to the God who creates something from nothing. I create faith in those who have none. That is what I did when I first called you to life. And now, I can generate love and forgiveness in you that you do not have on your own. I can create hope when nothing in your circumstances would justify such confident expectation. I can speak into the emptiness in your life and fill it with purpose and meaning.

So often I see my life only through the lens of what I lack. But because I belong to you, my life is defined by your fullness and sufficiency. I'm opening my life to your creative power, knowing I offer you nothing, but knowing that is not a problem to you . . .

I Will Give Back to You Everything Sin Has Ruined

They will rebuild the ancient ruins,
*   repairing cities destroyed long ago.*
They will revive them,
*   though they have been deserted for many generations.*
Isaiah 61:4

Sin ruins. That's why I hate it. Sin may have ruined many things in your life—your reputation, your relationships, your health, your happiness—but I will not allow your past to prevent you from experiencing all that I am preparing for your future. I intend to restore everything sin has ruined, both in this world and in your life. I intend to prove, through Christ, how much I can love ruined human beings.

You need not live looking over your shoulder at the rubble left in the wake of your life. Though you have sinned greatly and strayed from me, your sin has been nailed to Christ's cross, and my mercies are new for you each morning. From the rubble of your forgiven past I will build an edifice of my glory. I will even use you as a creative force to bring restoration to the world around you.

I know that all of the ways I seek to justify myself fall into a heap of ruins before you. I need what only you can provide. Revive me. Restore me. Renew me . . .

FEBRUARY 6 | 37

I Will Bless You as You Choose to Bless Others

Don't repay evil for evil. Don't retaliate with insults when people insult you. Instead, pay them back with a blessing. That is what God has called you to do, and he will bless you for it. 1 Peter 3:9

Hang this word upon the wall of your soul: *Bless*. When you are harshly and unfairly criticized—bless. When you are overlooked and underappreciated—bless. When you are intruded upon and insulted—bless. You will never regret responding to others' cruelty in a way that seeks to bless them, but you will certainly regret responding in like cruelty. As you respond by seeking to bless rather than blame or belittle, it will become obvious that you belong to me and that I am at work in your life, strengthening you for facing the assaults of the world.

I have called you to a life of giving and receiving blessing. And when you live in the world in this way, you will be rewarded. As you bless others, you will receive a blessing from me. As you bless the world, it will be both silenced and saved.

Your call to respond to being hurt by seeking to be a blessing forces me to my knees to ask for your power. Please make me a blessing today . . .

I Am Giving You a Heart to Enjoy Me

Whom have I in heaven but you?
I desire you more than anything on earth.   Psalm 73:25

I have given you so much in this world to enjoy, and I'm so glad you take pleasure in it. But what you genuinely enjoy reveals the deepest truth about you and matters forever. That is why I am giving you a heart to enjoy me above all else. If you try to live the Christian life with all of the right beliefs and practices but with no real passion for me, you'll find yourself continually frustrated and unfulfilled. I want something better for you.

Having faith in me is a good thing, but desire is the heartbeat of faith. Faith is power to enjoy Christ above all else in the world. Faith is believing not just what I can do but what I am worth.

I created you to glorify me by enjoying me above all else. I want you to desire me as an end in myself, not as a means to some other end. I will not be used. I will only be loved and enjoyed as the desire of your heart. I am claiming your heart as a sacred place of deepest love, where no one else may go.

Lord, all of my miseries flow from the mega-sin of treating you as a stepping-stone to something else. I want to love you as you define love . . .

Your Proven Faith Will Result in Much Praise

When your faith remains strong through many trials, it will bring you much praise and glory and honor on the day when Jesus Christ is revealed to the whole world.   1 Peter 1:7

I want you to see today's adversity in light of future glory—my glory that I intend to share with you into eternity. As you maintain a consistent grasp upon this glorious reality to come, its consoling power will strengthen you to endure your grim circumstances.

On that great day in the future there will be no quibbling complaints or lingering questions. Instead, there will be praise for the wisdom of my sovereign plan and your submission to it. There will be the glory of my perfect love and your reflection of it. And there will be honor for my sustaining power and your reliance upon it.

As you trust me, I will give you eyes of faith to see that day when your hard-fought perseverance will result in great glory. As you depend on me, I will give you ears of faith to hear me say, "Well done."

Go ahead and test me, Lord. Let the world get a glimpse of your goodness and glory through my enduring confidence in you . . .

I Will Heal You of Your Idolatry

*I will heal you of your faithlessness; my love will know no
bounds, for my anger will be gone forever.* Hosea 14:4

Because I love you, I want to deliver you not only from your
general problem with idolatry, but also from the specific, day-
to-day idols that consume you, control you, and cause conflict
with those around you. This won't happen in one sweep or
through one great spiritual experience. Instead, I am calling
you to identify and confess your idols one by one, and then to
cooperate with me as I steadily remove them bit by bit from
your heart.

This healing process will likely hurt. It hurts to see some
of the ugly obsessions of your heart brought out into the open
and severed at the root. It hurts to surrender some of your
most cherished desires that have become choking demands.
To bring healing, my Spirit will continue to press and prod
through layers of concealment, disguise, and justification.
Your idols will not give up their influence easily, but they are
no match for the healing power of my Spirit.

*I timidly open my heart to you, Lord, foolishly afraid that you
will take away something I've come to love. But I don't want to
linger any longer worshiping and sacrificing to false idols . . .*

I Have Given You a Secret Weapon to Fight Sin

You have no obligation to do what your sinful nature urges you to do. For if you live by its dictates, you will die. But if through the power of the Spirit you put to death the deeds of your sinful nature, you will live.   Romans 8:12-13

I am sending you on a search-and-destroy mission—to search out and then put to death the lingering sin in your life. But you're not on your own. In this battle I have given you a secret weapon that provides the power and the guidance you need—the Holy Spirit.

Experiencing my power is not mystical or subjective. The Holy Spirit clarifies and applies the objective Scripture to you, making it understandable to your sinful and finite mind. He gives you the strength you need to continually kill off sin in your life. Your part is not as simple as "Let go and let God" or "Just say no." Putting to death the deeds of the body requires your active obedience, empowered by the Holy Spirit. I am giving you the power of the Spirit to say no.

You've provided what I need to get rid of the ugly, depleting, defeating holdovers from my sinful nature. I'm opening up your Word so your Spirit can use it to point out my sin. Then I'm looking to you for the power to kill it off . . .

I Will Show My True Self to You

Moses said to God, "Suppose I go to the Israelites and say to them, 'The God of your fathers has sent me to you,' and they ask me, 'What is his name?' Then what shall I tell them?"

God said to Moses, "I AM WHO I AM."

Exodus 3:13-14, NIV

To know me, you must accept me on my own terms and not edit out the parts you don't like. If you try to change me, you'll dishonor me and deprive yourself of my goodness. But if you'll let me be God, you will discover that I am better than the designer god of your preferences.

I am not subject to the standards of others. I don't need anyone else to tell me who I am. And I am better than you think. If you'll say to me, "Show me your glory," rather than projecting your own God-preferences onto me, I will do it. The answer to this profound prayer is what you need more than all the seemingly significant items on your prayer list. This is the one thing that makes your life worth living—that you would see and savor the One True God.

I don't want a watered-down version or corrupted concept of you, God. I don't want to absorb ideas about you from my culture or from my own sense of need. Bless me with the weight of who you truly are . . .

I Have Loved You

"I have loved you," says the LORD. But you say, "How have you loved us?" "Is not Esau Jacob's brother?" declares the LORD. "Yet I have loved Jacob but Esau I have hated." Malachi 1:2-3, ESV

When the circumstances of your life tempt you to question my love for you, you must remember that I do not demonstrate my love by orchestrating your personal world in such a way that you can avoid suffering. When you find yourself tempted to hurl angry questions toward heaven, remember this: I chose to love you with free, sovereign, unconditional love. I set my love on you before you had met any preconditions or done anything that would endear you to me. I was under no constraint or moral obligation to love you. My love for you is the overflow of my infinite grace.

Why do I tell you this? To take away your presumption and remove every ground for boasting in yourself, to cut the nerve of pride that brags as though your salvation were owing to anything in you. The tragedy of a life is great love received with great ingratitude.

O Lord, how could I ever question the integrity or the expression of your love for me? I see your great love demonstrated at the Cross, and I am moved to humble gratitude . . .

I Am Writing a Love Story in Your Life

In all their suffering he also suffered,
  and he personally rescued them.
In his love and mercy he redeemed them.
  He lifted them up and carried them
  through all the years.   Isaiah 63:9

Your life is a love story being written by my own hand. And while some chapters will be more difficult or more interesting than others, visible in every scene, on every page, is my love for you.

My love for you determines the course and shape of your life and defines both who you are today and who you are becoming. You are enfolded in my love now and for eternity, and that love is the cornerstone you can build your life on. It is also your cushion from the blows life inevitably brings.

I love you simply because I have chosen to do so. I love you personally. I love you powerfully. I love you passionately. I love you when you don't feel lovable or lovely. I love you when no one else seems to care. Others may abandon or reject you, but I will always love you, no matter what.

How amazing that you have set your heart to love me when I know I am not worthy of such love . . .

My House Has Become Your Home

The one thing I ask of the LORD—the thing I seek most—is to live in the house of the LORD all the days of my life, delighting in the LORD's perfections and meditating in his Temple.
Psalm 27:4

How my heart sings when, with all the good things that call out for your attention and devotion, what you want most is me. This single-hearted devotion not only pleases me but will also bring you unending joy and pervasive peace.

Here in my presence, as you open yourself to my instruction, submit to my timing, and order your life around my priorities, you put me in my proper place—at the very center of your day-by-day existence.

As you make your home here, delighting yourself in me will not be a dry duty or a difficult discipline. It will flow naturally from your heart because of your regular exposure to my glorious perfections. As you meditate on my Word, you will receive the one thing you want most of all—more of me.

I'm making myself at home in your presence as I open up your Word and listen for your voice, Lord . . .

I Will Fill You Up

It was I, the LORD your God, who rescued you from the land of Egypt. Open your mouth wide, and I will fill it with good things.   Psalm 81:10

Sometimes you harbor dark suspicions about me, fearing that my intentions for you will only make you miserable. But remember what I've done for you—I am the God who has rescued you from a life of slavish devotion to what will ultimately destroy you. I have rescued you so that I might provide for you and do good to you.

Will you open yourself up to welcome my goodness? You can't just nibble at my edges and expect to be satisfied. It's wide openness to my Word, my ways, and my will that will fill you. Open yourself up to me by feeding on my Word, by welcoming my intimate presence, and by turning toward me and no other comfort when you feel angry or fearful or jealous or empty. No one else in all the universe can honestly say to you, "I will fill you." So trust me with no defensive preconditions. You only have to be open.

I open my mouth wide to your grace, in all its unfamiliar tastes and unexpected joys and sorrows. Widen my mouth so I can enjoy more of your goodness . . .

I Am Making You More like Me

All of us who have had that veil removed can see and reflect the glory of the Lord. And the Lord—who is the Spirit—makes us more and more like him as we are changed into his glorious image. 2 Corinthians 3:18

My Spirit is changing you. I'm making you into a clearer reflection of me. When people look at you, I want them to think you are looking more and more like your heavenly Father day by day. The more you look at me, the more you will look like me. You look at me as you read my Word and think about what I've said throughout the day. Then you look like me as you begin to live out what you have read. It becomes a part of you.

I have planted in every woman a desire to be beautiful and in every man a desire to be handsome, and really it has little to do with how you look on the outside. It is all about how well you reflect my beauty. Look at me, and let my Spirit make you more and more like me.

Spirit, change me. Give me eyes to see how beautiful you are. Then give me the grace I need to reflect your beauty that lasts forever, instead of my own that fades away . . .

I Am Worth the Wait

The Scriptures give us hope and encouragement as we wait patiently for God's promises to be fulfilled.   Romans 15:4

I know that you would rather I do things on your timetable. But I love you too much to conform to your agenda. I'm inviting you into mine. And sometimes that will mean that you have to wait on me. This is nothing new. Throughout history, people of faith have always had to learn to wait.

But I also know that waiting isn't easy. Waiting on me to act, to provide, or to heal is hard. But when you learn to wait patiently on me, something significant happens inside your soul. My promises become more precious to you and become the solid ground of your hope. You become more dependent on me, learning to trust that waiting in whatever frustrating, unproductive situation you are in will prove eternally valuable.

Wait for me. Watch for me to work. I will, when the time is right.

Lord, I am always in such a hurry for relief and resolution. Teach me to wait patiently, without complaint, calmly trusting that you will do the right thing at the right time . . .

I Will Welcome You

Dear brothers and sisters, we can boldly enter heaven's Most Holy Place because of the blood of Jesus. By his death, Jesus opened a new and life-giving way through the curtain into the Most Holy Place. Hebrews 10:19-20

There was a time when my presence was hidden behind a curtain in the Temple, and once a year only one priest could come into my presence. Sin separated my people from my holy presence. They had to relate to me from a distance.

But Christ has broken down that barrier so that you can come into my presence without fear of being consumed in my holy fire. The barrier was broken on the day—at the very moment—that Jesus died. I ripped from top to bottom the Temple curtain that had separated my people from me, and I threw open the doors to welcome you in. Now you can boldly approach my throne, confident that you will not be rejected but will be fully accepted and welcomed because of Christ.

I refuse to linger away from your presence, fearful of being exposed. You have opened up your abode to me and so I'm entering in, taking in the magnificence of your holy presence opened to sinners like me . . .

I Will Meet You in Life's Painful Places

*I was caught up to paradise and heard things so astounding
that they cannot be expressed in words. . . . So to keep me
from becoming proud, I was given a thorn in my flesh.*
2 Corinthians 12:4, 7

Plenty of people like to impress others with their accounts of
spiritual experiences. But I don't want you to seek after them.
It is not in spectacular spiritual experiences that you will have
your most significant spiritual breakthroughs. It will be in the
painful places, as you seek to make sense of your suffering and
submit to me in it, that you will find yourself relating to me
on a new plane.

What authenticates your relationship with me is not some
miraculous overcoming of life's difficulties, but your faithful
endurance in them. Your simple gladness in the setback will be
the greatest indicator of your deep connectedness to me. Your
life will be a living advertisement for the all-sufficient grace
available only through Christ. You won't feel cheated by the
setbacks; you'll know that you've been blessed.

*My prayers will no longer consist of efforts to convince you to
lubricate the gears of my perfect life. Instead, I want to redefine
my ideal life as following my crucified Savior in suffering
well . . .*

My Gospel Not Only Saves You, It Changes You

This same Good News that came to you is going out all over the world. It is bearing fruit everywhere by changing lives, just as it changed your lives from the day you first heard and understood the truth about God's wonderful grace. Colossians 1:6

Just as my gospel bore fruit in your life when you believed and were saved, it continues to bear fruit in your life as you are sanctified. Your life becomes more conformed to mine not when you try harder or do more, but when you believe better. Every part of your mind, heart, and life is transformed as you continue to feed on the Good News, believing it more and more deeply day by day.

As you believe better about my forgiveness, you find yourself filled with power to forgive. As you believe more deeply in the healing I am bringing to all creation, you find yourself demanding less of this life and expecting more of the next. As you believe more solidly that the righteousness of Christ has been imputed to you, gratitude swells up into more holy living.

Your gospel is at work in me, enabling me to live a life set apart to you. Every day I am discovering new implications and applications of the gospel . . .

I Will Not Reject Your Repentance

The sacrifice you desire is a broken spirit. You will not reject a broken and repentant heart, O God.   Psalm 51:17

I am not looking for you to pay for your sin. It has been paid for in full by Christ on the cross. But neither do I want you to trivialize, excuse, or defend your sin. I want you to be broken over it because you know what an offense it is to my holiness and what an abuse it is of my grace. This kind of brokenness will make you whole and healed.

The repentance I am calling you to is not a onetime thing; it is a way of life. You will never grow beyond being broken and contrite before me. As you walk with Christ, the Spirit will continue to show you areas of your life where you are headed in the wrong direction, calling you to turn toward me. I'm not looking for a particularly emotional experience of sorrow, although certainly sorrow will engage every part of you, including your emotions. Your genuine repentance will be evidenced by lasting change. The evidence that you have truly repented is that you will forsake the sin.

When I come to you honestly acknowledging my failure and humbly seeking mercy, you never turn me away . . .

What Satan Intends to Harm, I Will Use to Help

To keep me from becoming proud, I was given a thorn in my flesh, a messenger from Satan to torment me.   2 Corinthians 12:7

So often you want to nail down a singular source for your suffering. You wonder: Was it you, God, who did this to me? Did I bring this on myself? Or is there some evil force at work in my life? Paul's experience shows that what Satan sends to destroy your faith can, at the same time, be sent by me to develop your faith. What Satan inflicts in an attempt to make you turn away from me in resentment, I intend to use to strengthen you as you turn toward me in dependence.

Because you belong to me, your pain is not meaningless or random. It is purposeful. I intend to use it in your life for my own good purpose. I may not reveal that purpose to you, but that doesn't mean I don't have one.

The essence of faith is being confident in what you can't see. You might not be able to see how or when I am using your suffering for good, but you can still be confident that I will.

Instead of being so focused on who is to blame, I will begin to focus on welcoming you to work. Use the suffering in my life to keep me from sin . . .

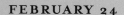

I Will Enter in as You Open Your Life to Me

Listen! It's the voice of someone shouting, "Clear the way through the wilderness for the LORD! Make a straight highway through the wasteland for our God!" Isaiah 40:3

In your life there are valleys of crushing disappointment, mountains of pride, and uneven ground and rough places of wrong thinking. As you open your life to me, you will find that I fill in valleys of sadness, bring down mountain strongholds of evil, and level out the rough places of your personality so that you can finally be who you want most deeply to be.

Your best days are still ahead. You have a future in Christ. And here's how you can prepare for it: Empty your hands of all rival comforts and securities so you can take hold of me. Clear away the obstacles of unrelinquished resentments and unconfessed sin. Give me open access to your mind as you meditate on my Word, and to your heart as you nurture new affections for me. You don't have to be perfect for me to bless you. Christ was perfect on your behalf. But you do have to clear away obstacles and open yourself up to me.

I'm opening up my life to your comfort, Lord, peeling away my false fronts, refusing to defend my internal barriers, welcoming you in . . .

I Will Lift You Up

Humble yourselves under the mighty power of God, and at the right time he will lift you up in honor.   1 Peter 5:6

I am not out to diminish you or make you mediocre. In fact, my intention is to make you glorious. But the way into this grander future may be surprising. You will not get there by exalting yourself, but only by humbling yourself before Christ. Though it goes against everything the spirit of this world tells you, the truth is that pride will ultimately humiliate you, while humility will result in great honor.

While pride uses my Word for its own purposes, humility reveres and submits to my Word. While pride defends and justifies, humility listens and responds to reproof. While pride is concerned with saving face, humility confesses sin.

I am a humble God who loves proud sinners. My grace will give you the power to bow low. As you humble yourself under me, you can be sure that the day will come when I will lift you up.

I have a lust for being noticed, a penchant for self-importance as well as self-pity. How I need your spirit of humility. Down low before you is where I belong. It is the place of real blessing . . .

I Have Put a Desire in Your Heart to Worship Me

I will make an everlasting covenant with them: I will never
stop doing good for them. I will put a desire in their hearts to
worship me, and they will never leave me.   Jeremiah 32:40

Oh, how I delight in doing good for you! I will never stop
doing good for my people. Out of my goodness I have
implanted in you the desire to worship me with abandon and
without pretense. As you worship me with your lips and your
life, reflecting my true worth to the world around you, you
experience my blessing.

You see, my goodness toward you is not that I make much
of you, but that I've implanted in you a desire to make much
of me. My love for you is expressed in giving you a heart that
longs to exalt me to a place of honor in your life. As you gaze
on my unfathomable worth and beauty, your focus is drawn
away from your issues, your preferences, your anxieties, your
sorrow. You find that you are drawing your very life from
mine, an abundant life that will last forever.

I know that my heart has turned toward you only because you
have implanted that desire. How good you are to draw me close
and bind me to yourself for all eternity . . .

I Will Give You the Gift of Eternal Life

For the wages of sin is death, but the free gift of God is eternal life through Christ Jesus our Lord.   Romans 6:23

Sin is a cruel and deceptive master. It promises pleasure, and when people obey, at first it feels like freedom. But in reality, sin only enslaves and depletes. It takes, but it does not give. In fact it takes and takes and takes, earning the sinner the only wage it ever pays—death. Sin seduces its slaves to disobey me and then disappears, leaving sinners to perish.

But I am the Master you were made to serve. I do not take from you, nor do I need you to work for me. I intend to give to you—to give and give and give. And what I give is gifts, not wages.

There will never be a day when I will stop giving more new joys to my people. I will never run out of gifts, ceasing to be a great Giver. It will take an eternity for me to exhaust the riches of my kindness toward you in Jesus Christ.

I have clearly earned eternal death, yet in your generous grace you have given me the free gift of eternal life. I know that I will spend eternity enjoying more and more of the wonders of your grace . . .

I Will Give You the Grace to Go against the Crowd

You can enter God's Kingdom only through the narrow gate. The highway to hell is broad, and its gate is wide for the many who choose that way. But the gateway to life is very narrow and the road is difficult, and only a few ever find it. Matthew 7:13-14

There is a comfort that comes from being in the majority, a sense of rightness from going along with the crowd. But that is not how things work in my Kingdom. I am not subject to the opinion of the majority.

In fact, huge numbers of people in the world are simply wrong about me and about what makes life worth living. They will not follow me or my ways, and they will surely come to a destructive end. But not you. You have set your course toward me on a road that is narrow and difficult and often lonely. I am giving you the grace to go against the crowd and to identify yourself with the marginalized, the rejected, the ridiculed. I am leading you toward the truth and away from what is popular. I am leading you to myself.

I often sense that I'm going against the grain. I value and desire different things than most people around me. And I know it's because you are at work in me, setting me apart for yourself . . .

I Grant Wisdom

Cry out for insight,
*   and ask for understanding.*
Search for them as you would for silver;
*   seek them like hidden treasures.*
Then you will understand what it means to fear the LORD,
*   and you will gain knowledge of God.*
For the LORD grants wisdom!
*   From his mouth come knowledge and understanding.*
Proverbs 2:3-6

How I love to see your heart that longs to do right, and your feet that want to walk in the path I have laid out for you! Do you think I will withhold the guidance you long for, the understanding of my Word that you read in search of knowing my mind? Of course not. But there are no shortcuts. Spend time in my Word. Spend time on your knees. The intensity of your search will be met with abundance of understanding. As you saturate yourself in my Word rather than snack on tidbits here and there, your questions will be answered, insight will be given, treasures will be revealed.

On my knees before you in my secret place, with your Word stretched out before me, I cry out to you for wisdom and insight. And again and again you give it to me generously . . .

I Am Shaping You into Something Beautiful

Does a clay pot argue with its maker? Does the clay dispute with the one who shapes it, saying, "Stop, you're doing it wrong!" Does the pot exclaim, "How clumsy can you be?"   Isaiah 45:9

Just as a potter spins a lump of clay on the wheel, pressing and forming it, transforming the shapeless clay into a work for his purpose, so I am shaping your life into something I can pour my own glory into. You can resist my shaping through rebellion or resentment, which makes you hard and unbending. Or you can be soft and moldable, open to whatever I want to do in and through your life.

You are still a work in progress, and I continue to refine you so that I can use you for a unique purpose in this world. I want to smooth out certain parts of your character. I want to redesign your inner life, reorganize your priorities, redirect the tendencies of your tongue, and rewire your thinking patterns. I am out to make something beautiful of your life, and the softer you are toward me, the more beautiful your life will become.

O Great Potter, shape me as you see fit. As only you can, mold me into a person you can use in this world . . .

I'm Equipping You to Help Those Who Hurt

He comforts us in all our troubles so that we can comfort others.
When they are troubled, we will be able to give them the same
comfort God has given us.   2 Corinthians 1:4

As I come to you and comfort you in your troubles, I do not
want you to become a reservoir of that comfort but a channel
through which my comfort flows into the lives of hurting
people all around you.

Just as I have met you and comforted you in the hard places
of your failures and losses, I want you to open your eyes to
see and open your arms to comfort people around you who
are experiencing failure and loss. I want you to channel the
comfort my Spirit has given to you as you've mourned the
death of the one you love into a determination to be the first
person on the doorstep of the friend who loses a loved one.
I want you to share with others how I've been faithful to you
in the hard times, so that they will believe that I will be faithful to them, too.

Lord, use the hurts in my life to open my eyes to the hurting
people around me whom I never noticed before. As you give me
strength, I will boldly enter into their pain and walk through it
with them . . .

I Have Defined True Relevance for You

In the beginning the Word already existed.
 The Word was with God,
  and the Word was God.   John 1:1

The world stands back from me, seeking to determine if I have any relevance for modern life. But you know better. You know that the significant question is not how I might be relevant to you, but how your thoughts and your life are relevant to me. I am God. I define relevance and reason and meaning.

The Word that expresses my creative genius, the Word that called everything into existence, is not a blind force. Ultimate reality is not physics; it is a Person—a living Person who existed before anything else. He takes priority over everything else, and everything else depends on him for its existence. This Person was face-to-face with me throughout eternity past, distinct from me, yet one with me—near to me, communing with me, enjoying me, and being enjoyed by me. What or who could be more relevant to you than the One who made you and all there is?

In Jesus you visited my world personally, lovingly, sacrificially, redemptively. From you I find a home for all of my restless wanderings in this world, and a center for life's meaning . . .

I Will Give You the Strength to Be Meek

Blessed are the meek, for they will inherit the earth.
Matthew 5:5, NIV

As my gospel goes to work in your life, you will become a person who is marked by meekness. While meekness sounds like weakness, really meekness is strength that is under control—strong but submissive. It is not necessarily people with certain personality types—shy or unopinionated—who are meek. Strong, outgoing people can be meek as they submit their strength to me. You can become increasingly meek in spite of your natural desires to go your own way and get your own way.

Meekness goes against everything the world says about getting what you want. You think you can get what you want by standing up for yourself and looking out for your own interests. But meek people are the ones who are going to inherit the earth. The meek will get what will last forever.

Jesus, you have shown me what true meekness looks like in your strong submission to God's plan that led you to the Cross. Without that spirit of meekness I will never be able to submit to your work in my heart and your plan for my life. So may your gospel go to work on me, making me truly meek . . .

My Salvation Is a Gift, Not a Reward

God saved you by his grace when you believed. And you can't take credit for this; it is a gift from God. Salvation is not a reward for the good things we have done, so none of us can boast about it.   Ephesians 2:8-9

I am a giving God, and I make myself known through my gifts. The most important things in life—forgiveness, a right relationship with me, acceptance into my family as my child, life that never ends, spiritual understanding, the transforming power of my Spirit, the promise of my blessing now and forever—these are all gifts that I give to those I have chosen to be mine. I don't negotiate. I can't be bribed or manipulated. There is nothing you can do to get these things from me apart from my choice to give them.

My gift of salvation is not a reward for your performance, and neither is it payment for services rendered. It all hangs on grace. I have saved you by my grace because you believe.

You, Lord, are the Giver of all I have received. There is no room for pride in accomplishment but only thanksgiving that you placed the gift of salvation in my outstretched hand of faith . . .

I Will Show You How to Lose

You suffered along with those who were thrown into jail, and when all you owned was taken from you, you accepted it with joy. You knew there were better things waiting for you that will last forever. Hebrews 10:34

Nobody likes to lose. And it can be hard to imagine that for my sake you could lose what you value, and that you could accept that loss without complaint or resentment, but with joy. There's only one way that can happen. The secret to being able to lose what is precious to you and still have joy is knowing that there are better things waiting for you that will last forever.

Do you know, deep in your soul, that what I have prepared for you is really better? Will you nurture that belief by relishing my promises of inheritance, reward, responsibility, glory, joy, abundance, intimacy, and peace? As you do, you'll find that you can live free from the fear and greed that could have kept you chained to security, safety, ease, and comfort. You'll be able to lose, knowing that because of all that awaits you in my presence, you will not lose out.

All of my losses for your sake here on earth remind me that something better is waiting for me in heaven when I see Christ . . .

My Grace Will Be Enough for You

I was given a thorn in my flesh. . . . Three different times I begged the Lord to take it away. Each time he said, "My grace is all you need."   2 Corinthians 12:7-9

Often when you come to me asking for relief, what I really want to give you is more of myself. I want you to discover that the grace I will provide to you is enough to endure the pain I do not remove from you.

I know that you look around at the suffering some people experience and think that you simply could not handle it should it come your way. And you're right. I have not given you the grace you need for those circumstances because you don't need it. But know this—if I allow that thing you can't imagine into your life, I will also give you the grace you need to endure it faithfully. You can face an uncertain future with confidence that whatever you need to stay faithful and joyful in the midst of your storm will be provided to you—in the timing, quantity, and form in which you need it.

I'm finding that I have more confidence and less fear than I had before. I completely believe that whatever you allow into my life, you will also give me the grace to endure faithfully . . .

I Will Give You the Glory You Seek

To those who by patience in well-doing seek for glory and honor and immortality, he will give eternal life; but for those who are self-seeking and do not obey the truth, but obey unrighteousness, there will be wrath and fury. Romans 2:7-8, ESV

All have sinned and fallen short of my glory. Yet it is still true that I created you for greatness and stature and significance and impact. That is why you long to be admired and to stand out, and why it hurts so much when you are degraded and trivialized. You yearn for significance, and that is good.

It's not wrong to long to be special. What's right or wrong is not the longing, but how you go about getting it satisfied. Will you turn to me for this? Will you anchor your sense of glory and accomplishment in the glory of the Cross and the accomplishment of my resurrection? I have made you and I am shaping you for eternal greatness. I am not out just to make you nice, but to make you surprisingly and delightfully formidable.

My destiny in you, Lord, is far greater than I could ever conceive or achieve on my own. Make me glorious in your likeness. Let me boast only in you . . .

I Will Deliver You from Dryness

He said to me, "Speak a prophetic message to these bones and say, 'Dry bones, listen to the word of the LORD! This is what the Sovereign LORD says: Look! I am going to put breath into you and make you live again!'" Ezekiel 37:4-5

I know your soul sometimes feels dry, like you are just going through the motions with me. My people have always gone through dry, desert times—Moses put up with the complaining, sinful people in the desert for forty years; Elijah sat under the broom tree in utter discouragement when the Israelites turned to Baal. Even Jesus was tempted in the dry desert wilderness.

When you are in a dry place, see that I am preparing to use you. Here you will learn how to trust me and delight in me in spite of what you feel. As you persevere in the dryness, you will break through into times of refreshing in me. I offer myself as living water to all those who look to me in their dryness.

My spirit is dry, Lord, with no vigor for pursuing you or serving you today. I need your Spirit to breathe life into me. Flood me with your abundant life and joy . . .

I Will Not Be Defined by You

The LORD answered Job from the whirlwind: "Who is this that questions my wisdom with such ignorant words?"   Job 38:1-2

I do not direct the course of things according to your desire. In my plan there are other motives that operate entirely outside of your preferences. The problem comes because you fancy yourself the main object at stake; it is your happiness, your honor, your future—and a little of me added in. According to your idea, you are the center of things, and I am here to make you happy. My almightiness is solely to serve your interest. This is an idea of me that is false through and through. It turns the order around, so that you seek to put yourself in the place of God and make me into your servant.

You may think that you want a God who will fit neatly into the box you've created for me. But you don't want a God who conforms to you. You don't want a God who is afraid to defy you or mystify you. You want to know and be known by the real God.

For the first time I'm feeling what it is to confront the living God. Purify my knowledge of you, God, so that I will not settle for anything less than the real God . . .

I Am Changing the Way You Think

Don't copy the behavior and customs of this world, but let God transform you into a new person by changing the way you think.
Romans 12:2

I know you feel constant pressure from the culture you live in, which seeks to squeeze you into its mold. It feels awkward to go against the tide of opinion, to see everything through the lens of a different perspective. But don't give in to the pressure to conform.

Instead, let me bless you by transforming and renewing your mind from within, where my Spirit dwells. Let my Word inform your thought process, and let my perspective shape your priorities. As you live differently, treasuring Christ and putting your whole hope in him, you'll prove to yourself and to the world around you that my plans for my people are good. There will be something different about you—you'll look and think and talk more and more like my Son.

I simply don't want to think the way I have in the past and the way those around me who have no love for you do. Lord, change the way I think about what will make me happy, what is truly important, what will bring me lasting joy . . .

I Am Building You into My Spiritual House

You are coming to Christ, who is the living cornerstone of God's temple. He was rejected by people, but he was chosen by God for great honor. And you are living stones that God is building into his spiritual temple. 1 Peter 2:4-5

I am making you part of something that is bigger than you are as an individual, something more important than your own agenda. You are a living stone in the house I am building to live in forever. My house is made up of believers coming together as my covenant people to worship me—living stones being placed side by side on the solid foundation of Christ.

I have no interest in building a bigger or better rendition of a dead temple. What good is an earthly temple to the Lord of heaven and earth? I am building a house of living stones who will worship me in spirit and in truth, offering up the sacrifices of a broken spirit and a contrite heart, songs of praise, and deeds of kindness. I am building my church, the people in whom and with whom I will dwell forever.

How is it that you could use me, as unfit as I am, to build the house that you—Most High God—would want to live in? Surely the grace that has come to me in Jesus is greater than I know . . .

I Have Set Out Boundaries for Your Protection

The LORD our God commanded us to obey all these decrees and to fear him so he can continue to bless us and preserve our lives, as he has done to this day. Deuteronomy 6:24

My rules were not given to diminish your life but to add to it. They are a gift to you, an expression of my love toward you.

In my commands I have given you a light that points out what will hurt you, a set of boundaries that will keep you close to me, and a clear standard for judging your thinking and behavior.

The Ten Commandments are the most complete description of absolute good that has ever been given. Through them you learn that you must bend your life to conform to my goodness rather than redefine good to fit your crookedness. My law is like a mirror that shows you who you really are—a lawbreaker who needed a perfection you could not achieve on your own and a forgiveness you could not earn. And that is what you've been given in Christ Jesus.

Your law would leave me hopeless if I did not know that Christ fulfilled the law perfectly in my place. So now your law is my guide and keeper, showing me the way to abundant life . . .

My Spirit Is Filling Your Heart with My Love

We know how dearly God loves us, because he has given us the Holy Spirit to fill our hearts with his love. Romans 5:5

I want my love for you to move beyond a cerebral fact you accept to a felt reality you experience. The Holy Spirit makes this happen supernaturally. It is his work, not yours. I have sent my Holy Spirit on a mission from heaven to enter your heart to assure you of my love and to help you experience it.

This experience of my love is self-authenticating—a subjective basis for assurance that my love for you is real. But it is not a vague, out-of-body experience or ecstatic condition produced by a lack of critical thinking. This subjective experience has objective content. Your experience of the love of God is a response to the story of my love for you, demonstrated in history in the death of my Son for your redemption. As you fill your mind with the truth of what Christ has done, my love becomes a felt reality at the core of your being.

Holy Spirit, you are illuminating the glory of God's love for me in the work of Christ, opening my eyes to see and my heart to feel the ravishing reality of such infinite love . . .

Obeying My Commands Brings Joy

Praise the LORD! How joyful are those who fear the LORD and delight in obeying his commands. Psalm 112:1

Oh, how it makes me happy to see the delight you take not only in reading my Word, but in obeying it. You are discovering that my commands are meant for your joy, not to confine you or control you. And because you delight in obeying my commands, you are living in that place of joy and peace and abundance that I've intended for you all along.

Those who persist in rejecting my Word and making their home far away from me and my commands are right to live in fear of my judgment. In fact, they should be very afraid. But your fear of me is much different. You have no cause to be afraid of me. Instead, you have a holy reverence for me that creates in you a longing to live a life that pleases me. Because you fear me, you not only have joy now, but you can be confident that this joy will only increase into eternity.

Praise you, Lord! The better I know you, the more I fear you. And as my reverent fear of you increases, so does my joy . . .

I Have Given You a Gift to Use to Serve

God has given each of you a gift from his great variety of spiritual gifts. Use them well to serve one another.   1 Peter 4:10

I have given you a gift—not a material one, but a spiritual one. This gift is not intended primarily for your personal enjoyment, but for you to employ in service to others. My gift will enable you to give yourself away to those around you in ways that will effectively strengthen their faith and walk with me.

My Spirit distributes my gifts, and he alone decides which one each person should have. He has given you a gift that is just right for you, and you must fan it into flame. I want you to use what I've given you to serve others—if profuse wisdom, use it to serve someone who needs wise counsel. If helping others, use it to serve someone who needs your practical assistance. If teaching, use it to gently correct someone who does not understand my Word.

Holy Spirit, wake me each day wondering how I can help other people become stronger in their faith. Show me how I can fan this spark of a gift into a raging fire that burns for your glory, faithfully serving the needs of others . . .

I Will Not Abandon You

No, I will not abandon you as orphans—I will come to you.
John 14:18

I hear your constant prayer asking me to "be with" you and those you care about as you face the daily realities of life in this world. And while I love for you to ask me for what I've promised to provide, sometimes this request reveals that you doubt this foundational promise of my covenantal relationship with you. Perhaps you seek some physical evidence of my presence, some miraculous demonstration that you are not forgotten. Hear my call to find the assurance you need, not in a supernatural experience but in my sure and certain Word. When you feel abandoned, on your own, do not listen to those feelings. Instead, rely firmly on my promise.

I have already answered your request to be with you even before it leaves your lips. I am with you, but more significantly, I am in you. I have come to you as Helper, Counselor, Comforter, Spirit of Truth, Advocate, and Teacher to dwell not only with you, but in you.

You have so fully and so freely given yourself to me, even giving me the Holy Spirit to live within me. I know that I am never truly alone . . .

I Will Wipe Away Your Tears

You keep track of all my sorrows. You have collected all my tears in your bottle. You have recorded each one in your book.
Psalm 56:8

As you live in this world that is broken, your life does not go untouched by pain and sorrow. Perhaps you think that if you had real faith you wouldn't have to feel sad. But your tears do not reflect a lack of faith. Tears are a tool I use to bring healing in your life.

I do not discount or dismiss your tears. They are precious to me because you are precious to me. In fact, at the culmination of human history, I will personally wipe away all tears. I won't awkwardly ignore them or suggest that if you really had faith you wouldn't cry. No, I will lovingly wipe them away. Not only that, I will also remove all of the sorrow that caused those tears in the first place. My plan for the future is to destroy forever the evil that has brought you so much pain. Then I will live forever with you in a place I have lovingly prepared—a place where there will be no more tears.

It's hard for me to grasp that you are sad with me. Give me the faith to see you now beside me and to see a future in which your hand will wipe away my tears forever . . .

I Have Broken Down the Barriers

Let us come boldly to the throne of our gracious God. There we will receive his mercy, and we will find grace to help us when we need it most.   Hebrews 4:16

The enemy would like to keep you thinking that you are unworthy and I am unapproachable—all with the intention of keeping us apart. But don't believe it. I have broken down every barrier that would keep you alienated from me. You are not worthy on your own to come to me, but Christ has made you worthy. So come. Come quickly. Come continually. Come confidently. You can draw near knowing that you're wanted and welcome, not cowering in shame or wondering if you'll be rejected.

I'm inviting you not to a throne of judgment but a throne of grace. I do not deal in intimidation but in mercy. You can draw near with confidence that you will be accepted, wanted, and provided for. You will receive mercy for your past failures and grace to meet your present and future needs.

I will not waste one more minute on the fringes of real relationship with you, believing the lie that I have everything to fear from you rather than everything to gain from you. So I come boldly, in need of your grace . . .

I Have Chosen to Bless You through a Book

All Scripture is God-breathed and is useful for teaching,
rebuking, correcting and training in righteousness.
2 Timothy 3:16, NIV

Of all the ways I could bring you my blessing, I have chosen to bless you through a book. Will you receive this blessing today by immersing yourself in my holy book?

The struggle you face today is not how you will refute all of the voices in the world who deny or twist or diminish my Word. The struggle is closer to home—simple distraction, diversion, and busyness. Hundreds of channels to watch and websites to view and interests to pursue fill your life with so much distraction that you have little stillness for thinking deeply about my Word and thereby entering deeply into my presence.

I have set my Word before you so that you can stop running. Sit down, think, and open up to the things that will matter forever. You must cultivate your capacity to enjoy my Word. Discuss it with your friends, chew on it, memorize it, go deep with it, and find yourself truly blessed.

Forgive me, Lord, for seeing your Word as an obligation or
assignment rather than the blessing it really is . . .

I Have Set You Free from Angry Passions

Let all bitterness and wrath and anger and clamor and slander be put away from you, along with all malice. Be kind to one another, tenderhearted, forgiving one another, as God in Christ forgave you. Ephesians 4:31-32, ESV

As long as you live in this world, people will wrong you. But my love for you is too big to let you linger in the hell of holding a grudge. In hell, grievances are kept fresh by the passions of envy, self-importance, and resentment. But as a citizen of heaven, as one who has experienced great forgiveness, you are operating in a new atmosphere. You can no longer say that while your sins are forgivable, someone else's sins against you are not. You experience a love that comforts you better than self-pity as you lay down your injuries at the foot of Christ's cross.

How you treat other sinners tells the truth about your relationship with me.

Too often I have loved my hurt more than your healing. But I'm not going to keep simmering in resentment. Your forgiveness calls me to surrender my angry passions to love, to enjoy the gracious gladness of being a forgiven sinner . . .

I Have Given You Earthly Pleasure to Enjoy

Since everything God created is good, we should not reject any of it but receive it with thanks. For we know it is made acceptable by the word of God and prayer.   1 Timothy 4:4-5

Everything I have created is good. So you can receive this earthly life—with its pleasures of a fine meal, a hilarious joke, a sparkling lake, and a passionate romance—with thanksgiving. As you look beneath the surface, you will find in your everyday life continual proof of my goodness.

The holiness I desire is not found by denying yourself the simple pleasures of this life. As you receive my gifts with simple thanks, your enjoyment is lifted to the level of the holy. Holiness can fill every moment of every day of your life as you receive grace upon grace from me with a heart filled with gratitude.

Yes, everything I have created is good, but it is not ultimate. It is all but a taste of my ultimate and eternal pleasures. Only I am ultimate. Only I can satisfy your desires fully and forever.

As I enjoy the fantastic wonders and simple pleasures of your world, my heart is moved to worship and thanksgiving . . .

I Want All of You

You must love the LORD your God with all your heart, all your soul, and all your strength.   Deuteronomy 6:5

I could settle for whatever scraps of devotion you find it convenient to offer me, but I love you too much for that. I intend to bless you with a far richer life.

I want your heart to beat with passionate love for me; I want your soul to find its home in my presence; I want your strength to be drawn from me. This is what will make you deeply and eternally happy. So I am calling you away from lesser lovers to pure-hearted pursuit of me. I'm calling you away from soul-stealing distractions to soul-feeding devotion to me. I'm calling you away from all of those activities that sap you of energy to pursue our relationship so that you will be strengthened for your walk with me.

Christ alone has loved me with all of his heart, soul, and strength. So abide in him. He will work in you to generate this kind of single-hearted devotion.

You, God, are glorious. You're most worthy of my passionate love, my worship, my energetic pursuit . . .

Salvation Comes from Me

My salvation comes from the LORD alone.   Jonah 2:9

Your salvation is not something you accomplish. It is my work from first to last.

I am the great Architect of salvation, its sovereign source and loving initiator.

I determine the timing and method of salvation. I select the objects of my salvation. I do the work of salvation.

Salvation cannot be earned from me or manipulated out of me. It must be received from me as a gift and recognized as coming through the Cross of Christ.

I have saved you from futility, from slavery, from an eternity of punishment. I have saved you to meaning and freedom and an eternity of pleasure. I have saved you from death and saved you for life.

I am the Great Savior, and my salvation is certain and secure. You need no other Savior, no other source for salvation. I have saved you. I am saving you. You are saved and safe.

Salvation comes from our God, who sits on the throne, and from the Lamb! . . .

I Find Joy in Doing Good for You

They will be my people, and I will be their God. And I will give them one heart and one purpose: to worship me forever, for their own good and for the good of all their descendants. And I will make an everlasting covenant with them: I will never stop doing good for them. Jeremiah 32:38-40

I find joy in doing good for you, my child. Will you trust me to determine what is good and to provide it for you in my timing, on my terms? While I welcome you to pour out your wants before me, how I long for you to become so confident in my good purposes toward you that you will no longer beg me to accomplish your predetermined positive outcomes.

As you become more convinced of my goodness and my commitment to your good, worship will move from a determined discipline to a natural outflow and expression of our love relationship.

You are a God who does not withhold from me. You have put a desire in my heart to worship you, which is your greatest good toward me . . .

I Will Show You a Way Out of Temptation

The temptations in your life are no different from what others experience. And God is faithful. He will not allow the temptation to be more than you can stand. When you are tempted, he will show you a way out.   1 Corinthians 10:13

Your enemy, Satan, continually assaults you with temptations—the same temptations he has been using to capture sinners in his trap since he slithered into the Garden of Eden, tempting Eve to find her satisfaction apart from me, to pridefully usurp my place, and to question my goodness and provision.

But you are not at Satan's mercy. I have set boundary lines that he cannot cross. I will never allow him to push you too far or press in so hard that you will be unable to say no. And I am always available to show you a way out, a way to escape from the trap of his lies. In fact, what he intends to use to defeat and diminish you, I will use to strengthen you. What he intends to use to tempt you to turn away from me, I will use to train you to turn toward me in fresh dependence.

While I am full of excuses, you are faithful. You keep opening up new doors of blessing just when I think I am trapped by temptation . . .

I Will Give Your Life Back to You in Abundance

If you refuse to take up your cross and follow me, you are not worthy of being mine. If you cling to your life, you will lose it; but if you give up your life for me, you will find it.
Matthew 10:38-39

Your enemy would like to convince you that I cannot be trusted, that I will deplete and disappoint you, and that I make too many demands on you. But the truth is that only I can be trusted to surpass your expectations and supply true satisfaction. I do not come to you making demands on your life, but showing you how you can truly have your life.

But you must be willing to wait. You must be willing to trust that everything you let go of in this life will be returned with even more in the next. You must see that your present life isn't worth protecting.

My call is not for you to turn to me so that I can enhance your current lifestyle and protect your emotions. I call you to die to yourself and follow me. Then I will reward you beyond all you can ask or imagine.

Your Cross serves as the warning label on the Christian life. But it is also the key to eternal joys. Following Christ will cost me everything, but it will also give me everything . . .

I Will Silence Your Accuser

The accuser of our brothers and sisters has been thrown down to earth—the one who accuses them before our God day and night. And they have defeated him by the blood of the Lamb and by their testimony.   Revelation 12:10-11

Your enemy is always at work, reminding you of your sin and accusing you continually before me. Satan takes perverse pleasure in reminding you again and again of your past failures so that you will indulge in endless and hopeless introspection. He wants you to focus on your merit—or lack thereof—instead of Christ's.

Such rehearsal of the sin you have repented of does not come from the ministry of my Spirit. The conviction I bring draws you away from yourself and toward me in repentance, flooding you with relief as you know that I accept you. Self-condemnation draws you down into yourself and away from me. It makes you afraid and distrustful of me, trapping you in relentless self-loathing and unbelief. But I do not condemn you. I accept you because of Christ.

I cannot conquer the Accuser and his damning accusations by rehearsing my good works, but only by confident testimony of the blood of the Lamb spilled in my stead . . .

I Will Be Your Strength When Your Spirit Is Weak

Whom have I in heaven but you? I desire you more than anything on earth. My health may fail, and my spirit may grow weak, but God remains the strength of my heart; he is mine forever.   Psalm 73:25-26

When you have descended into despondency, when fatigue and anxiety have done damage to your body and soul, when you've run out of resources, you will find that I am still with you, offering myself to you. I am the solid strength to which you can tether your life in the storm, and I am yours forever.

When the bottom drops out of your life and Satan colors the shock wave of the experience with black hopelessness, do not yield to it. Open my Word and let its light shine into your darkness. My Word revives souls that have been wrung out by difficulty and confusion. Believe my promises. Receive my promised peace. Tether yourself to my strong presence. Surround yourself with godly companions who know and love my Word. Fight unbelief with rugged faith. Rest your soul in my sovereign wisdom.

When I am at the very bottom, with no more physical, emotional, or spiritual resources left for the fight, you are still right beside me, reminding me of your love and your promised help . . .

I Will Give You a Responsive Heart

*I will give you a new heart, and I will put a new spirit in you.
I will take out your stony, stubborn heart and give you a tender,
responsive heart.*   Ezekiel 36:26

How is your heart today? Is it defensive, stubborn, resentful,
hardened? Not if you are abiding in me. I have much better in
mind for you. When you turned to me, I removed that stony,
stubborn heart that could not be broken over the sorrow of
sin. And in its place I have given you a heart that is tender
toward me and responsive to me.

This means that now your heart can be broken by the
things that break my own heart. Your heart can beat with a
passion for what pleases me. Your new heart cannot ignore my
conviction or disregard my instruction for long. Instead, as you
catch fresh glimpses of my glory, your heart worships, and as
you discover deeper goodness in my gospel, your heart melts.

*My heart sings to you on this new day, Lord, only because you
have given me this new heart. Because it is tender, I can be
hurt, but I can also feel joy . . .*

I Will Come Close to You

Come close to God, and God will come close to you. James 4:8

It can be so easy to let distance come between us. Your busyness can keep you from lingering in my presence. Your entertainment choices can sap your appetite for my Word. Even your work for me can become a substitute for intimacy with me. And before you know it, there is an awkward chasm that has come between us.

The enemy whispers that there's nothing wrong with this place away from me, that you'll be more comfortable here. But don't listen. You are mine; you belong to me. I have a far better life for you that is found only in my presence. So turn toward me. Take a first step in my direction. You will find that my arms are open to welcome you into the place of intimacy and oneness that I've intended for us to share since before the day you were born.

I never intend to wander away from you, Lord, but I do. So once again I am turning toward you. And I know that you will not refuse me or shame me for my wandering but will welcome me in . . .

I Will Not Let Sinful Impulses Dictate Your Life

You also should consider yourselves to be dead to the power of sin and alive to God through Christ Jesus. Do not let sin control the way you live; do not give in to sinful desires. Romans 6:11-12

I know that you don't always feel dead to sin—that you often feel quite alive to it, invigorated by its passions. But your feelings do not tell you the truth. The truth is that because you are united to Christ, you are now dead to sin. The connection has been cut off. All ties have been severed. Now you are alive to me. We are deeply connected as my life flows into yours.

As you begin to see yourself as dead to sin and alive to me, you'll find power to resist sin's desire to draw you back into its grasp. Seeing yourself this way is not a mind game or merely pretending. It is how you live out this new reality.

Sin is a power, not just an act. And the power of sin wants to control your life. But because you are united to Christ, the power of sin has been broken in your life. Sin is no longer the boss. You can say no. You can say good-bye to old habits and long-term tendencies.

I have severed all ties to my old life of chasing after sin, and I am now joined to you . . .

I Have Made a New Covenant with You

The Lord Jesus took some bread and gave thanks to God for it.
Then he broke it in pieces and said, "This is my body, which
is given for you. Do this to remember me." In the same way,
he took the cup of wine after supper, saying, "This cup is the
new covenant between God and his people—an agreement
confirmed with my blood. Do this to remember me as often
as you drink it."   1 Corinthians 11:23-25

I have established my Supper as a reminder and proclamation of the new covenant I have made with my people. As
you remember what Christ has done and feast by faith on his
finished work, I want you to savor the promises of the new
covenant. As you ingest the bread, remember my sacrifice for
you. As you put the cup to your lips, taste the sweetness of my
covenant commitment to you—my promises to forgive your
sin, to make my will your delight and not just your duty, to be
your God and make you my own people. Savor the pardoning
and purifying power of my blood shed for you.

I remember, Lord. Your covenant with me is precious to me. As
I eat and drink, my soul is fed by faith in what Christ's broken
body and spilled blood have secured for me . . .

I Have Given You a Gospel Celebration

For every time you eat this bread and drink this cup, you are announcing the Lord's death until he comes again.
1 Corinthians 11:26

It is easy, in fact completely natural, for you to focus your attention on yourself—how you're doing, what you're learning, how your prayer time is going, how you have avoided or fallen into that same old sin. So I have given you a celebration, a meal, that will help you turn your thoughts away from yourself and focus them on Christ—on his sinless life, his substitutionary death, his triumphant resurrection, his glorious ascension, his righteous reign, and the promise of his return.

Your heart is in such need of this gospel celebration, this regular reminder. When you fail, you need the comfort of being reminded that Christ died for the very sin you just committed. When you succeed, you need the humbling of being reminded where your strength comes from. When you wonder if your life will ever change, you need to be reminded that my Spirit is at work within you, cleansing you and re-creating you.

As I eat the bread and drink the cup, I proclaim the incredible merits of your life and the saving power of your death not only to the world around me, but to my very own soul . . .

Christ Lives in You

My old self has been crucified with Christ. It is no longer I who live, but Christ lives in me. So I live in this earthly body by trusting in the Son of God, who loved me and gave himself for me.   Galatians 2:20

I'm happy to tell you that the old you has died—the old you who lived only to please yourself, the old you who was not inclined to me. When you put your faith in Jesus, you became united with him. His death became your death. You could say that you died two thousand years ago on the day that Christ died. But you would also have to add that you came alive again on the day Christ rose from the dead, because just as his death is your death, his resurrection is also your resurrection.

And here's the best part about being crucified and risen with Christ: because you have already died, you will never truly die again. Though your body will one day succumb to death, the essence of who you are will live forever and will one day be rejoined to your resurrected body.

Since my old self is dead, my old selfish ways are gone. The way I used to think about things is gone. My pride-fueled arrogance is gone. You are replacing my old life with your resurrection power and life . . .

I Have Poured Out Your Punishment on Another

He was wounded for our transgressions;
    he was crushed for our iniquities; . . .
the LORD has laid on him
    the iniquity of us all.   Isaiah 53:5-6, ESV

My goodness to you is not that I will allow your sin to go unpunished. I do not look at you and say, "You're guilty, but I am overlooking it because I am so nice." Neither do I say, "You're not that guilty after all; you're really a very nice person." Niceness is a cheap human substitute for real goodness. I see you as you are and must say, "You are guilty." But I also say, "There is no sin you can commit that I cannot forgive."

The goodness of my just punishment and merciful forgiveness come together at the Cross of Christ. I enforced my perfect justice on Christ so that I might unleash my abundant forgiveness on you.

Every last sin will be punished. I will by no means simply write it off. I punish sin in one of two ways: either personally, in an unrepentant sinner's own experience in hell, or substitutionally, in Christ's experience at his Cross. And because your punishment has been laid on Christ, you have no need for fear.

Your goodness to me, Lord, is that you do not demand my blood in payment for my sin, but give your own . . .

In Life and Death, You Are in My Hands

Jesus shouted, "Father, I entrust my spirit into your hands!" And with those words he breathed his last.   Luke 23:46

It is natural to be afraid of death. But if you are in me, you are no longer living life or facing death in a natural way. Instead, my Spirit inside you enables you to respond in a supernatural way. You can face death with confidence—confidence that everything I've promised is true and that everything you've placed your hope in is real. This confidence comes from being convinced that nothing can separate you from my love—not even death.

Find your rest in my promises and your peace in following the example of Christ, who cried out from the cross, "Father, I entrust my spirit into your hands!" Entrust your spirit into my hands too. Shout from the depths of your soul with the psalmist, "My future is in your hands!"

Your life is in my hands, and your death is in my hands. The deaths of those you love are in my hands. And because of that you can rest, knowing that when you are mine, there is no safer place to be.

I'm entrusting myself into your care now, in the days ahead, and for my eternal future . . .

I Provide Power over Death

No one can take my life from me. I sacrifice it voluntarily. For I have the authority to lay it down when I want to and also to take it up again. John 10:18

Every spark of life began with me. I am the life giver and life sustainer. I made humans out of dust and breathed life into them. My Spirit can give you life that will not end when your body goes back to the dust.

I am not waiting until some future date to start giving you this never-ending life. A new quality of life begins for you the moment you come to me. If you have me, you have life, even though death is all around you. Your life flows from mine, and my life cannot be snuffed out. I'm inviting you to rest in who I am—life itself—and in what I've promised you—rich, satisfying, unending life.

Trusting my promises takes faith. But I'm not talking about blind faith or a leap of faith. You find the foundation for faith in the reality of Christ's resurrection. And I am promising you that same death-defying, life-giving power.

I am staking my life and my death on your power over death. Because of you, I can face death without fear, confident that unstoppable life is on the other side of death . . .

You Will Live, Even after You Die

Jesus told her, "I am the resurrection and the life. Anyone who believes in me will live, even after dying. Everyone who lives in me and believes in me will never ever die. Do you believe this, Martha?" John 11:25-26

Because you live in me and believe in me, death will never be able to separate you from me. So even though your current physical life will one day come to an end, that will not be the end of you. You will be with me until that day I reunite your soul with your body, one that is glorified, perfected, and resurrected like mine.

When you hear me tell you that I am the resurrection and life, however, know that I am not merely speaking of something I will do in the future. I am telling you who I am now. I stand before and beyond the limits of birth and death to grant you abundant, unending life.

I do believe, Jesus, that you are the resurrection and life. I believe that you can be trusted to infuse my present and my future with overflowing, unstoppable life. Because you have been made alive, I know my life can never be extinguished . . .

I Hold the Keys to Death

Don't be afraid! I am the First and the Last. I am the living one. I died, but look—I am alive forever and ever! And I hold the keys of death and the grave.   Revelation 1:17-18

I am in charge of life and death. I hold in my hand the keys to the place of the dead. No one goes there unless and until I open that door. This means that no matter what the doctor says, you will live exactly the number of days I have ordained for you. This means that when that person you loved died in an awful accident, it didn't catch me by surprise. It means that even though it seemed like the one you loved died much too soon, it was really right on time.

This means you can surrender all the if-onlys that taunt you in your thoughts—if only he had gone to the doctor earlier, if only I had warned her, if only I had been a better witness, if only I had seen the signs. It means that you don't have to surrender the one you love to an unknown, uncaring nothingness. You can rest, knowing that the person you love who knows Jesus is safely in my care and under my loving control.

I don't have to be afraid. I can surrender my need to always be in control, confident that you not only hold the keys, you hold me as well . . .

I Offer Hope on a Grand Scale

Look! I am creating new heavens and a new earth, and no one will even think about the old ones anymore.   Isaiah 65:17

Is your hope big enough and imaginative enough to take in what I intend to do in this broken-down world and your pain-ridden life? Do you find yourself wanting to reduce my grand plans to what may be shortsighted and manageable to you in the here and now?

The hope I provide is on a grand scale. It offers the prospect of personal intimacy with me forever in a renewed world of peace and righteousness. This hope is both personal and universal. My ultimate answer to your longing for my intervention is nothing less than a new heaven and a new earth that begins now as I make you into a new creation in Christ.

You do not have to work to keep this grand hope alive. Instead, this hope will keep you alive.

Every day of life in this world tempts me to throw my hope away. Too often my hope is too small. The future of the world is already taking place inside of me as you make me new . . .

I Will Share My Happiness with You

The LORD your God is living among you. He is a mighty savior. He will take delight in you with gladness. With his love, he will calm all your fears. He will rejoice over you with joyful songs. Zephaniah 3:17

I am not a God who is aloof or emotionless. I am not strained and serious with a furrowed brow. I am happy—radiantly, outrageously, eternally happy. Nothing and no one can frustrate my happiness.

And you need to know that you make me happy. Because of Christ, I not only accept you, I enjoy you! I do not only tolerate forgiven sinners; I take delight in you. I haven't just made room for you in heaven; I have made room for you in my joyful heart. I pursue you in your restlessness, receive you in your sinfulness, hold you in your brokenness, free you from your lovelessness, and rejoice over you in your unworthiness. How can I rejoice over you with such joy? Because I see you through my Son—my dearly beloved Son who brings me great joy. He has made you clean and good and holy.

How good you are to share your happiness with me. I know the day is coming when I will enter into my Master's happiness and share your joy forever . . .

I Am Not Settling for Self-Improvement

Jesus replied, "I assure you, no one can enter the Kingdom of God without being born of water and the Spirit. Humans can reproduce only human life, but the Holy Spirit gives birth to spiritual life."   John 3:5-6

I love you too much to settle for doing a simple work of self-improvement in your life. When you first came to me, you needed more than a little fine-tuning here and there. What you needed was something as radical as being reborn from above. You needed to become a new person in your essential being. My Spirit called into existence what was not there previously.

   This work of my Spirit is not explainable or controllable, but it is discernible and traceable. Once you were dead to my goodness. But now my Spirit has quickened your spiritual senses so that your soul thirsts for me, so that the one thing you most desire is to gaze upon my beauty, so that you find your greatest pleasures in my presence.

The miracle you have accomplished in my life is so profound, I can't understand it. You have entered into the depths of my being with new life. I continue to open my life to your Spirit as you impart life—new life that comes only from you . . .

I Am Comforting You with the Truth

This is my comfort in my affliction, that your promise gives me life.   Psalm 119:50, ESV

I know you long for comfort when life is hard, when people are unkind or uncaring. You look for answers, hope, and tenderness. Turn to my Word and you will find me there, speaking truth that dispels the voices inside you and around you that speak only words of despair.

Come to my Word. Don't look for a quick fix, taking words out of context that seem to promise what you are hoping to get from me. While this may give you a temporary injection of pleasant thoughts, it will only leave you disillusioned and disappointed when I do not live up to what you've mistakenly assumed I have promised you. Instead, come to my Word seeking to understand the big picture of what I am doing in the world, and therefore in your life. Here is the truth that provides your great comfort: You are not on your own, but you belong to me body and soul. Your sins will never be held against you. Satan cannot have you. I will preserve and protect you. In life and in death, you are in my hands.

Only your truth provides the deep and lasting comfort I crave. I'm turning to you, opening up your Word . . .

I Have Canceled Your Debt

He canceled the record of the charges against us and took it away by nailing it to the cross.   Colossians 2:14

How do you see me? What do you think of me? Do you think I am up in heaven keeping track of all your wrongs against me? I know that is what you do with yourself and with those around you, but I am not like you.

Don't think that I am not interested in moral punishment or the settling of scores. I am too just to overlook the evidence. But the case against you—the file folder with all of the facts, names, dates, photographs, and all of the damning evidence against you—has been nailed to the Cross. Jesus suffered the penalty for your guilt, and now you are clear with me.

So will you live in the light of this reality, with the outrageous joy of one who has been set free from death row? I have settled the score through Someone else, Someone who took your place as your substitute at his Cross. I was strict in enforcing my righteous judgment. I demanded everything—but not from you.

Sometimes this gospel truth seems too good to believe and I go back to the prison of guilt, shame, and fear. But your truth, Lord, is setting me free . . .

I Will Protect You from the Evil One

Holy Father, you have given me your name; now protect them by the power of your name. . . . I'm not asking you to take them out of the world, but to keep them safe from the evil one.
John 17:11, 15

Jesus prayed for you. He prayed that I would keep you safe from the evil one. Jesus asked this because he knows the devil wants to destroy you. Satan prowls around like a roaring lion looking for someone to devour. Satan brings suffering in an effort to diminish your faith, he brings temptation in an attempt to deceive you, and he brings doubt about my love and goodness to try to estrange you from me. Satan's goal in this world is to keep you alienated from me and claim you as his own for eternity.

But Jesus has prayed for you, asking me to protect you from the evil one, so you are not at Satan's mercy. I have answered Jesus' prayer with a resounding yes! All those who are in Christ are safe from the damning power of the evil one.

While Satan may win a battle or two in my life, he will never win the war against my soul. Jesus has prayed for me, and I am protected . . .

I Will Lead You through All of Your Sufferings

God called you to do good, even if it means suffering, just as Christ suffered for you. He is your example, and you must follow in his steps. 1 Peter 2:21

A life of following me will make you durable in difficulty. Hard times will come and comforts will go while you still stand firm in following me.

I'm not suggesting that you are able to follow me because you are strong. I'm saying that my power at work in weak people gives them the courage they need to speak truth in the face of criticism and opposition. My Word taking root in foolish people gives them the wisdom to recognize what is true and what is false. My grace at work in suffering people gives them the ability to face hardship, loss, and disappointment and not lose their joy.

With your hope firmly grounded in the gospel, you can face anything. I will lead you through all of your sufferings into all of my joys.

I don't want my joy to be so fragile, Lord. I don't want my confidence and contentment in you to be so vulnerable to my circumstances. I hear your call to suffer, and I believe your grace at work in me will strengthen me for it . . .

I Am Giving You a New Motivation

We have been released from the law, for we died to it and are no longer captive to its power. Now we can serve God, not in the old way of obeying the letter of the law, but in the new way of living in the Spirit. Romans 7:6

Oh, yes, I want you to obey me. You will be blessed as you live according to my ways. But you need not obey me out of slavish fear, always afraid that the slightest slipup will make you vulnerable to eternal punishment. You are not obligated to obey my law as a way of avoiding my wrath. Christ perfectly obeyed every facet of the law in your place and offered himself as your substitute, so I have already poured out on him every drop of the wrath that you deserve. I have only mercy left for you.

The obedience I want is a response to my love and grace. In fact, all other obedience always degenerates into doing penance or trying to avoid punishment. If your obedience is not motivated by love for me, it will always be motivated by love for yourself.

What a relief that I do not have to worry about measuring up anymore, because Christ measured up in my place. When you look at me, you see his perfections and pour out more of your love . . .

I Will Save the Best for Last

They will see his face, and his name will be written on their foreheads. Revelation 22:4

I have shown you so many good things—my favor, my mercy. I have granted you forgiveness, gifted you with insight, and flooded your life with my own joy. But there is so much yet to come.

The day is coming when disappointment and death will be no more. In their place will be abundant healing and fruitfulness, rich beauty and satisfaction. The day is coming when I will show you what will bring your greatest joy and satisfaction. I will show my face to you. You will see the radiance of my countenance smiling down on you, welcoming you, rewarding you. You will see the beauty of my character like never before—clearly and completely.

I am giving you abundant life now and in the days to come. But you can celebrate in knowing that I will save the best for last—when you will see my face.

I have been marked as yours, Lord. How I long to see the beauty of your face smiling as you look me in the eye and say, "Well done." . . .

I Want to Expand Your Life

Wherever your treasure is, there the desires of your heart will also be.   Matthew 6:21

This is a world of hustling, building, working, creating, reaching, saving, and hoarding. And the energy that drives it all is often anxiety. You worry about paying the bills—having enough plus a little more. Fearing that I will fail you, you over-focus on yourself. You think you'll make a difference later by giving, but right now you need to save. Later, when you can afford it, you'll get around to what your heart longs for.

It is easy to talk yourself into a fearful contraction of your life, saying no to wonderful opportunities. But I want to talk you into a bold and blessed expansion of your life. I want you to get free of worry, so that you can throw yourself into the thrill of advancing my Kingdom. I want you to invest in what will last forever. I have not promised to underwrite a self-centered lifestyle with my provision. But I will provide what you need to accomplish what I've called you to do.

I know that I can live in practical commitment to you because you live in practical commitment to me. I don't have to grovel any more at the dictates of the idol Money . . .

Your Savior Intercedes for You

Because Jesus lives forever, his priesthood lasts forever. Therefore he is able, once and forever, to save those who come to God through him. He lives forever to intercede with God on their behalf.   Hebrews 7:24-25

Just as you could not save yourself, you cannot keep yourself saved. And just as Christ employed his power to save you, he is using his power to keep you. He is interceding for you even now before my holy throne.

Your future salvation depends not only on the finished work of Christ on the cross, but on the active and ongoing work of Christ as your High Priest forever and ever. This very day you are being saved by the eternal intercession of Jesus. He is your Advocate in the only court that counts. He is your connection for access into my very presence. He pleads for me to accomplish my perfect will in your life, praying that you will walk in the truth and complete the work that has been entrusted to you. He asks that the truth of my Word will teach you and refine you, so that you will become holy as I am holy.

How I need an Advocate, a Mediator to plead my case before you, God. You have given me the only intercessor I will ever need—Christ himself. So hear his pleadings and prayer on my behalf . . .

I Am Worthy of Your Costly Worship

Whenever the living beings give glory and honor and thanks to the one sitting on the throne . . . they lay their crowns before the throne and say, "You are worthy, O Lord our God, to receive glory and honor and power."   Revelation 4:9-11

I am preparing a crown for you as a reward for your faithfulness when circumstances tempted you to give in to doubt or rebellion. The crown is your reward for perseverance when you faced ridicule or persecution, even death, because of your love for Christ. It is the gift I will give you for loving me more than the things of this world.

This crown will not be a mere piece of jewelry you will thoughtlessly part with. It will be too precious. Yet the day is coming when you will lay down your crown before my throne willingly, gladly, joyfully. On that day, your sacrifices won't seem so sacrificial, your suffering won't seem so significant, because Jesus is so beautiful, so compelling, so worthy. It won't seem costly to you to lay down your crown because you'll see the full reality of Christ's unimaginable worth.

Lord, you supply the faith, the perseverance, and the courage— everything that will earn a crown. It all came from you and I want to give the glory back to you . . .

I'm Using My Word to Work in You

All Scripture is inspired by God and is useful to teach us what is true and to make us realize what is wrong in our lives. It corrects us when we are wrong and teaches us to do what is right. God uses it to prepare and equip his people to do every good work. 2 Timothy 3:16-17

Whenever you read the Bible and you learn something about me, or see something about yourself that needs to change, you are being blessed by me. I am giving you the gift of understanding the most important truth in the universe: how I will save people who don't deserve it. And I am showing you how you can receive the most valuable gift in the universe—salvation—which comes only by trusting me. You will hear lots of voices today claiming to tell you the truth. But test everything you hear against what I have said in my Word. I'm using it to prepare you to make a difference in this world for my sake.

Speak to me, Lord, through your Word today. Teach me what is true and correct me where I'm wrong . . .

I've Given You a New Nature to Go after Me

You have no obligation to do what your sinful nature urges you to do. For if you live by its dictates, you will die. But if through the power of the Spirit you put to death the deeds of your sinful nature, you will live.　Romans 8:12-13

I'm well aware of what your sinful nature urges you to do even though you now belong to me and have been given a new nature. That old sin nature wants to rob you of the abundant life only I provide. Every day your new nature is doing battle against the sinful cravings of your old nature. It perseveres and pushes toward everything that is holy, upright, perfect, and pure. Its instincts all run toward perfect holiness.

Your old nature does not care to pray, but your new nature prays as readily as you breathe. The old nature murmurs and complains, but the new nature sings and praises God from an impulse deep within. Your old nature goes after what made it happy, trying to get you to forget the new taste you have developed for holiness, but your new nature goes after what pleases me.

I am covering my ears to the lies of my old nature and welcoming your power to put it to death . . .

I Will Establish My Kingdom in Your Life

[Jesus] said to them, "When you pray, say: 'Father, hallowed be your name, your kingdom come.'" Luke 11:2, NIV

My Kingdom doesn't come into the world or into your life like a military overthrow that takes power by force. It comes as a small seed that must be planted in order to blossom. It comes as you welcome my authority into deeper recesses of your life. My Kingdom exists wherever my rule and reign have been established.

Because authority is so often misunderstood and misused in the world, perhaps you fear the impact of my authority in your life and so resist giving me free rein. But you need not be afraid. My authority is of a heavenly nature. I use it to serve and to give life, not to control or coerce. I use my authority to work for your good and cause you to flourish, not to make you miserable or to diminish you. The best days of your life are those in which my Kingdom authority breaks through into your heart, claiming more of it for myself.

What a joy it is to live in this world under your loving authority, with you as my King and my Father. May your Kingdom come in my life. Rule over my passions and preferences. Overrule my opinions and overcome my prideful resistance to your ways . . .

I Will Never Stop Loving You

Long ago the LORD said to Israel: "I have loved you, my people, with an everlasting love. With unfailing love I have drawn you to myself." Jeremiah 31:3

You've been hurt and disappointed by a friend too many times, and so you've decided the relationship is over. That's because your love has limits. You are human—changeable and unfaithful—and even though you want to love others well and faithfully, you fail.

But I am not like that. My love is not like human love; it has no limits. My love never gives up, never loses faith, is always hopeful, and endures through every circumstance. You can be confident that I will never stop loving you in all of the best ways. And when you wonder if my love is deficient because I've allowed something hard or painful in your life, think again. Instead of looking at my love through the lens of your difficult circumstances, choose to look at your circumstances through the lens of my unfailing love. You can be sure that no matter what happens, I am loving you in it and through it.

How can you know me so well and yet love me so faithfully, so purely, so completely? This is a holy mystery that I will accept and enjoy into eternity . . .

I Will Lead You for Your Benefit

He lets me rest in green meadows;
    he leads me beside peaceful streams.
    He renews my strength.
He guides me along right paths,
    bringing honor to his name.   Psalm 23:2-3

As your Shepherd, I cannot let selfish ambitions or sinful appetites become the driving forces in your life. My honor is at stake in the way I lead you, and so I must lead you in the way of holiness. When you stray onto paths that will take you away from me, or when wolves of compromise and complacency threaten to drag you away, I will bring you back to my fold where I will care for you, rule over you, counsel you, and instruct you in wisdom.

My Word will be a light to your path and a lamp to your feet. The day will come when you will look back over your life and see that I was there guiding you to your appointed end, giving you strength to persevere in saying no to those things that looked so appealing and so harmless but would have taken you far away from my loving care.

Lord, you are the beginning and the end of all my righteousness.
Your grace is my starting point and your glory is my
destination . . .

I Will Send You Where You Want Most to Go

They will go away into eternal punishment, but the righteous will go into eternal life. Matthew 25:46

Don't let anyone convince you that there is no such place as hell. Because it is so horrible, many have concluded that a loving God would never send people to such a place. And in a sense, I do not send people to hell. People receive what they chose during life—either to be with me forever, worshiping me, or without me forever, worshiping themselves. Hell is simply a person's freely chosen path going on forever. When people want to get away from me, in my infinite justice I send them where they want to go.

Certainly I do not want people to go to hell. That is why I provided a way of salvation. The soul that centers its life on me and my glory need not fear the fires of hell, but can look forward to ever-increasing joy.

What a great sadness it is to me that some people I care about, who have sought their whole lives to get away from you and your control, will finally be separated from you. And what a great comfort it is to me to know that I will go where I want most to go, never to be separated from you, but to be comforted by you into eternity . . .

There Is Always More of Me to Discover and Enjoy

O LORD my God, you have performed many wonders for us. Your plans for us are too numerous to list. You have no equal. If I tried to recite all your wonderful deeds, I would never come to the end of them. Psalm 40:5

No matter how far you go with me or how much you discover of me, there's always more to know and enjoy. In your pursuit of me, you are like a mountain climber struggling to reach the top of a mountain peak, only to discover that there are more amazing mountain peaks left to climb.

When you find yourself bored with my Word, the problem is not with the Bible. If you fill yourself with the cotton-candy entertainments and endeavors of this world, you will dampen your appetite for more of me. But if you persist in seeking after me, I will never stop revealing myself to you in richer and clearer ways.

May I never say to you, "Lord, I'm full. I've seen all of you I want to see; my love for you is as deep as I want it to go; my confidence in your promises is as serious as I want it to be; I've been changed as much as I want to be changed. I have as much of you in my schedule, my thoughts, and my heart as I need— and as much as I want." Keep giving me more of yourself . . .

I Have Saved You from Foolishness

People who aren't spiritual can't receive these truths from God's Spirit. It all sounds foolish to them and they can't understand it, for only those who are spiritual can understand what the Spirit means. 1 Corinthians 2:14

The people I consider foolish are not necessarily unintelligent or unable to understand. Rather, they have no sense of what is valuable and what is worthless. But I have saved you from such foolishness and made you wise unto salvation.

On your own, you were foolish; you couldn't see how valuable Jesus is. But the Holy Spirit invaded your value system so that you could see his true worth. You went from being bored by the Bible to enjoying my Word. You went from seeing yourself as the center of the universe to seeing me as worthy of all your worship. You went from seeking after pleasurable experiences to finding your greatest happiness from abiding in me. The Spirit enabled you to see how worthless a life is outside of Christ, and how precious it is to have him.

Thank you, Spirit, for taking away my foolish heart and giving me a heart of wisdom. I'm trading in what is worthless and temporary for what will be satisfying and worthwhile forever . . .

I Have a Harvest of Blessing for You to Reap

You will always harvest what you plant. Those who live only to satisfy their own sinful nature will harvest decay and death from that sinful nature. But those who live to please the Spirit will harvest everlasting life from the Spirit. So let's not get tired of doing what is good. At just the right time we will reap a harvest of blessing if we don't give up.   Galatians 6:7-9

I have seen the seeds that you plant. You sow seeds of contentment as you say no to the temptation to believe the lie that you need one more thing to be happy. You sow seeds of peace as you refuse to give in to the temptation to criticize and complain. You sow seeds of generosity as you give even when you have needs of your own. You sow seeds of humility when you turn the spotlight on someone else instead of on yourself.

Oh, the beauty that is blossoming in your life as these seeds take root and grow. Every choice you make to please the Spirit enhances the harvest of blessing you are sure to reap.

Don't let me grow tired, Lord, of choosing and doing what I know will please you . . .

Your Whole Body Can Be Used for What Is Right

Do not let any part of your body become an instrument of evil to serve sin. Instead, give yourselves completely to God. . . . So use your whole body as an instrument to do what is right for the glory of God. Romans 6:13

There is a war going on for control in your life. The enemy wants to use your body to betray you and belittle me, so you must give your body to me. As you give me increasing authority in your life, you will discover that every part of your body can be used to bring me glory.

Instead of giving your mind over to cynicism, think deeply about the truths in my Word. Instead of feasting your eyes on what is degrading, allow me to open your eyes to hurting people all around you who need to be loved. Instead of listening for the latest gossip, tune your ear to hear the sound of my voice. Instead of using your tongue to criticize, use it to bless, affirm, and encourage. Instead of giving your heart to trivial affections, give it wholly to me. This is the abundant life I have for you—using every part of your body to do what is right.

I know I do not have to give in to what sin calls my body or my mind to do. Instead, I'm giving my whole self—my body, my mind, my will, my emotions—to you, to do what is right . . .

I Will Water Your Parched Soul

O God, you are my God; I earnestly search for you. My soul thirsts for you; my whole body longs for you in this parched and weary land where there is no water.   Psalm 63:1

I know the world has a way of draining the life out of a person. All of life's demands, its difficulties, and its disappointments take their toll and leave you longing for refreshment.

As your longing leads you to me, I will refresh you. My promises will renew your hope. My grace will invigorate your resolve. My Spirit will comfort your hurts. As you earnestly search for me by listening to me through my Word and sharing your life and concerns with me through prayer, my river of delights will flood your soul.

The water I give to those who come to me becomes a fresh, bubbling spring inside you, giving you eternal life. So drink deeply of me. Savor the living water I've provided you in Christ.

My God, again and again I come to you all dried up from living in the desert of this world, and you refresh me and fill me with your living water . . .

I Have Opened My Arms to You

*Come to me, all of you who are weary and carry heavy burdens,
and I will give you rest. Take my yoke upon you. Let me teach
you, because I am humble and gentle at heart, and you will
find rest for your souls. For my yoke is easy to bear, and the
burden I give you is light.*   Matthew 11:28-30

Can you see me in your mind's eye when you hear these words?
Can you see me opening my arms to you, waiting to envelop
you, providing a safe place for you to make yourself at home?

When I tell you to take my yoke upon you, I'm not trying
to put you to work. I'm inviting you to share the yoke that
is also around my neck. I am offering to shoulder the load as
you connect yourself to me. I will do the heavy lifting of the
burden that is pressing in on you, crushing you.

And when I say, "Let me teach you," hear my heart, which
is humble and gentle. I don't bark orders or drill you for the
perfect answer. I will impart my way of living, my way of
understanding, my way of loving as you come and abide in me.

*I see your arms open wide to me, Lord, and I want to fall into
them and rest . . .*

I Have Made You My Child

God decided in advance to adopt us into his own family by bringing us to himself through Jesus Christ. This is what he wanted to do, and it gave him great pleasure.   Ephesians 1:5

My precious child, I am so glad to call you mine. Long ago I decided to adopt you into my own family by bringing you to myself through my Son. Now my Spirit is in you and you can come to me and call out to me—not as some distant deity, but as your papa, your daddy.

Because you are my child, you can walk confidently in this world, knowing that my thoughts toward you are always loving, my actions toward you are always kind. And my discipline of you is always for your good.

So do not let yourself operate in this world and interact with me as an orphan. You need not try to manipulate me to get what you need. I am your Father, and I know your needs before you ask. I will supply your needs according to my great riches.

Papa, how good it is to know that I have not been left on my own. I belong to you, and you will take care of me . . .

I Am Blessing You by Being Fully God to You

Oh, how great are God's riches and wisdom and knowledge! How impossible it is for us to understand his decisions and his ways! For who can know the LORD's thoughts? Who knows enough to give him advice? Romans 11:33-34

Have you considered just how much I know? My knowledge encompasses the past, the present, and the future. I know every event that has ever happened and ever will happen at every level of existence, including actions, thoughts, and motives. I am also wise. Wisdom is more than knowledge; it is knowing what to do with the knowledge you have and directing that knowledge to the highest and most moral ends. So while you should want to understand and try to understand what I am doing in history and in your life, you must confess your utter inability to probe the depths of my infinitely wise determinations.

While some are arrogant enough to suggest they would run this universe quite better than I do, the God you serve is not so weak as to need advice. I am sufficient enough in myself to have no need of tips to improve on my plan for salvation. I am blessing you by being fully and wonderfully God to you.

Rather than being frustrated by your inscrutability, I worship you for your great wisdom that knows no bounds and has no needs . . .

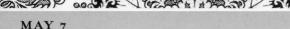

I Am Jealous for You

You must worship no other gods, for the LORD, whose very name is Jealous, is a God who is jealous about his relationship with you. Exodus 34:14

If I were not so passionate about you, I would not care when I see you investing your best energy in something else, turning your attention somewhere else, or giving your heart away to someone else. But I am jealous about my relationship with you. I am not out of sorts or irritable because of envy; rather, my jealousy is an expression of my passionate, exclusive, protective love as I rightly guard what belongs to me. I want to guard our relationship from anything or anyone who would come between us.

That is why I discipline you—as a way of regaining your heart, not as a means to cast you away. I discipline you to remove whatever keeps you from enjoying my love, so that you will be free to love me more fully and faithfully. Indeed, I will arrange circumstances of my own choosing to bring you to your senses and into my embrace.

As the unique, incomparable, only living God, you have made exclusive claims on me and have the right to a monopoly on my love . . .

I Have a Better Day Prepared for You

The day you die is better than the day you are born.
Ecclesiastes 7:1

When you were born, you began a short, fading, and uncertain life. But on the day you die, you will enter into unending life that cannot be diminished or extinguished. You were born into a world marked by disillusionment and disease, a world of sin and vanity and trouble. But the world you will enter upon your death will be perfected, awash in light and joy, without any mixture of sin and sorrow. While you live now in a world of fading pleasures, you will awaken to a world of substantial, durable joys. While death will take you away from all of your earthly possessions, it will impart to you a more glorious inheritance.

And while you are surrounded in this life by people whose hearts are full of hateful lusts and selfish dispositions, the inhabitants of the world to come will all have been made righteous. Only what is excellent and lovely will reign in their hearts. My image in you will be complete; all sin will be perfectly abolished. The holiness that is now just a spark will be a flame so that your soul will shine forth as the sun in my Kingdom.

Christ, it is you, and you alone, who will make the day of my death better than the day of my birth . . .

I Will Guard Your Heart and Mind

Don't worry about anything; instead, pray about everything.
Tell God what you need, and thank him for all he has done.
Then you will experience God's peace, which exceeds anything
we can understand. His peace will guard your hearts and
minds as you live in Christ Jesus.   Philippians 4:6-7

You are not meant to live with a sick feeling of fear simmering
in the pit of your stomach. I do not want anxiety to squeeze
the joy out of your life. I want you to live in peace, free of
the worry that wants to rob you of rest. Because you belong
to me, you can turn those panicked thoughts into prayers,
confident that I will hear. No concern is too small for me to
care about, and no situation is too big for me to handle. My
peace will take up residence in your heart, guarding it from
attacks of fear. My peace will rule your mind so that worries
will be subject to the truth of my Word.

　　Though I've thrown open the door to this beautiful place
of peace, you must choose to enter in. Release your concerns
to me and let me carry them. Capture each anxious thought
and turn it into prayer.

As I make my home in you, Lord, you are taking up guardian-
ship of my heart and mind. I'm realizing that I don't need to
worry . . .

I Am Empowering You for What Is Truly Important

When we place our faith in Christ Jesus, there is no benefit in being circumcised or being uncircumcised. What is important is faith expressing itself in love.   Galatians 5:6

Do you want to know what really counts with me? It is not going through the motions of religiosity or doing your duty. What counts with me is faith—authentic, rugged faith that goes to work in your inner life and comes out in the form of love not only for me, but for others.

I'm not suggesting that you must add a layer of loving works to your faith. I'm saying that the kind of faith that truly counts with me is faith that by its nature produces love—accepting love for the unlovely, patient love for the demanding, costly love for the needy, generous love that is really an overflow of your love for me. This kind of love for others proves that your faith in me is the real deal—that it is living, justifying faith.

When I have deep compassion for someone who is hurting and patience with someone who is difficult, I recognize that it is your gospel at work inside me, making me into a person who loves like you do . . .

Because I Love You, I Must Discipline You

Joyful are those you discipline, LORD, those you teach with your instructions. Psalm 94:12

If I had not set my saving love on you, you would linger in your sin, far away from me, wrapped up in yourself, deluded by the lies of the enemy, and doing whatever brings you pleasure for the moment. But you've been marked as mine, and so I will not let you go your own way, wandering away from me.

So that is why I discipline you. I know it looks like crushing disappointment, unwelcome interruption, frustrating limitation, and unjust hardship from your perspective. But you must see these things as tools in my loving hands that I am using to rub off the rough edges of your self-life and build up your spiritual muscles of perseverance and patience.

Don't resist my discipline. Don't resent it. Instead, welcome the blessing of being loved by me in this way.

Loving Father, teach me and train me. Don't let me ignore your discipline. Give me faith to trust you with it and eyes to see you in it . . .

I Will Do a Significant Spiritual Work through Your Prayer

I pray that your hearts will be flooded with light so that you can understand the confident hope he has given to those he called— his holy people who are his rich and glorious inheritance. I also pray that you will understand the incredible greatness of God's power for us who believe him. Ephesians 1:18-19

I have invited you into the privilege of talking with me—Lord of the universe, Lord of time, Lord over all—through prayer. So come to me, and let's talk. Let's talk about what really matters, leaving behind the superficial stuff, the surface issues. Prayer is a spiritual process toward a spiritual end. I want to do a deep work in your inner life, changing the way you think about things and cleaning up your character. So let's not settle for talking only about the shallow stuff.

Talk to me about your fears, invite me into your failures, and confess to me the things that bring you shame. Ask me for a deeper understanding of the hope you have in Christ and the power you have at work in your life. Open up your life for me to do a significant spiritual work.

As my prayers move from the superficial to the significant, I find myself inviting you to do no less than a deep, transforming, life-changing work in me . . .

My Mercy Never Reaches Its Limit

The faithful love of the LORD never ends! His mercies never cease. Great is his faithfulness; his mercies begin afresh each morning. Lamentations 3:22-23

Today is a new day, a new opportunity to find hope in the midst of hardship as you recall my commitment to you. Though yesterday's devastation and disappointment may have robbed you of your happiness and hope, you must inform your feelings and fears with what you know is true about me. And the truth you must embrace for all it is worth is that I am for you, not against you! My covenant fidelity and personal integrity stand firm and unflinching, securing your hope no matter what happened yesterday or what will transpire in the days to come.

You need not fear that I have abandoned you to the judgment that you rightly deserve. My mercy is too abundant, too persistent, too vigorous for that. My mercy goes the second mile, reaching into the darkness of your difficulty, filling your heart with fresh hope.

Forgive my doubts about your faithfulness that are fed by difficulty. Keep reminding me that I can trust you with my life . . .

I Will Supply All Your Needs

This same God who takes care of me will supply all your needs
from his glorious riches, which have been given to us in Christ
Jesus.   Philippians 4:19

I am supplying everything you need. I am your true source
and provider. And when you turn to me, asking me to supply your needs, you are not a bother. In fact, I love it when
you depend on me and look to me for what you need. That's
exactly the kind of relationship I'm looking for with you. So
today, when you enjoy a satisfying meal, know that I have
provided it for you. When you enjoy the companionship of
your friends and family, see them as a gift from me. When you
laugh, it's because of the joy I've given you. When you end
your day in the safety of your bed, that is from me too. And
don't forget that my greatest gift to you is myself. Without me,
all of my other gifts would be empty. But with me, they are
reminders of my loving care for you.

Jesus, I look to you today to supply all of my needs from your
own resources and riches. I believe that anything and everything
I need, you will provide . . .

I Will Cause Everything to Work Together for Good

We know that God causes everything to work together for the good of those who love God and are called according to his purpose for them. Romans 8:28

I have not promised that you will never have to suffer. But I have promised that your suffering will not be meaningless. It will not be wasted.

My promise to you is that I will cause everything in your life to work together for your good. And there is not one thing that falls outside of this promise—not suicide, not murder, not permanent disability, not divorce. It's not that these things are good. Clearly they are not. But because you love me, I will use the worst thing you can imagine for your ultimate good.

When the worst thing happens, it is hard to imagine what good could ever come out of it. This is where you must look to the Cross, the ultimate display of my ability to work all things—even the greatest evil and most cruel suffering of all time—together for good. If I can bring abundant good—the salvation of guilty sinners—from such evil, then you can be certain that I will do something good in and through the suffering in your life too.

It is hard for me to see how you will use the hard things in my life for my good, but I'm taking you at your word . . .

I'm Teaching You the Joy of Daily Dependence

Pray like this: . . . "Give us today the food we need."
Matthew 6:9, 11

When you pray, ask me for what you need today. Then tomorrow, come to me asking again. You see, I want you to learn to depend on me on a daily basis. While the world celebrates independence, I bless dependence. This is why, in the desert all those years ago, I sent manna to my people every morning and allowed them to store up only enough for that day. I was teaching them daily dependence, and I want to teach you to depend on me in this way too.

You will never find me lacking when you come to me. As you learn to depend on me more and more, and as you discover over and over again that I can be enough for you, you will begin to rest in my provision. You'll have less fear about whether or not I will show up tomorrow with what you need. You'll discover how blessed it is to hunger and thirst for me, and find me fully satisfying.

I have loved my independence, yet it has left me wanting, insecure, alone. So I'm turning to you in dependence, conscious that I am not a bother to you. Instead, you long for the relationship that comes with my daily request for what I need . . .

I Love You Too Much to Let You Wander

They defiled themselves by their evil deeds,
and their love of idols was adultery in the LORD's sight.
Psalm 106:39

I love you too much to allow for divided loyalties. My covenant calls for single-minded worship. I am like a husband who gets angry when someone else competes for the heart of my wife or when her heart trolls for other lovers.

So you must not commit adultery against me. Don't let your heart turn from me and go after other lovers in this world. Whatever lures your affections away from me with its deceptive attraction will not love you well. It will strip you bare and cut you in pieces.

As you forsake all other gods, cleaving only to me and living for my honor, you will find that my jealousy is not a threat but a comfort. You will rest in knowing that anything and anyone who threatens your good will be opposed with my divine power.

Lord, my heart is prone to wander. But as I begin to understand
your passionate commitment to me, my heart becomes more
tightly bound to yours, and all other lovers in this world lose
their appeal . . .

I Have Reserved Something for You

*We have heard of your faith in Christ Jesus and your love for all
of God's people, which come from your confident hope of what
God has reserved for you in heaven.*   Colossians 1:4-5

Most people around you live for what they can experience,
what they can accomplish, and what they can enjoy in this
life. But the gospel that has filled you with hope for more
does not primarily consist of directions for coping with life on
earth, but a redirection of your hopes toward life in heaven.
You no longer live for what is passing away, but for what will
last forever.

What will last forever in heaven will be Christ—visibly
displayed and admired and enjoyed by all who believed in
him in this life. In his presence, you'll be infinitely happy, not
because of what you've done for him, but because of what he
did for you at the Cross. Knowing that this is what you will
enter into the instant after your last heartbeat on this earth
makes you fearless in the world right now. Because you are
living for heaven, you don't have to cling to this life.

*My confident hope in heaven is freeing me from worldly self-
centeredness and self-pity, from fear and greed and bitterness
and despair and laziness and impatience and envy . . .*

I Look at the Heart

The LORD said to Samuel, "Don't judge by his appearance or height, for I have rejected him. The LORD doesn't see things the way you see them. People judge by outward appearance, but the LORD looks at the heart." 1 Samuel 16:7

How do you respond when you read that I can see your heart and know your true character? Does it fill you with confidence because you see your motives as pure and your desires for me as sincere? Or does it fill you with fear because you are well aware of how divided and dark your heart can be?

If you are in Christ, you have no cause for fear and no grounds for pride, but only a place for gratitude. I have seen your heart as it truly is, and I have made you my own. I see your mixed motives, I hear your arrogant words, and I read your critical thoughts. But I have no intention of rejecting you. I am working to change you. When I look at your heart, I see it in light of what it will one day be—purified, perfected, holy.

Lord, what a relief it is to know that when you look at my heart, you see the cleansing blood of Jesus applied to all its dark spots . . .

My Spirit Prays and Pleads for You

The Holy Spirit prays for us with groanings that cannot be expressed in words. And the Father who knows all hearts knows what the Spirit is saying, for the Spirit pleads for us believers in harmony with God's own will.   Romans 8:26-27

In your utter weakness and deepest despair, when you don't have the words or the will to ask for what you need, my Holy Spirit is praying for you with the kind of passionate groaning for which there are no words. And you can be confident that I will say yes to what the Spirit prays for you, because he always pleads for me to accomplish my perfect will in your life. He is at work in you, tearing down the walls of your resistance to my will.

I hear your prayers, asking for your path to be smooth and asking me to bless your plans with success. But that is not how the Spirit prays for you. He loves you too much for that. He prays that when your plans go awry and your efforts fail, your faith will not. He asks me to give you my best—more of my Spirit at work in the interior of your life.

Spirit, pray for me when I don't have the words. I want to desire God's will more than I want my own way. Tear down the walls of my resistance . . .

I Will Heal You

I am the LORD who heals you.   Exodus 15:26

I am Jehovah-Rophi, the Lord who heals. Healing is not just something that I do; it is my very nature, reflected in my name. I am the source and sustainer of life itself. So in your sickness, look to me. I want to heal you.

And I mean really heal you—not just heal your body temporarily, but heal your spirit, soul, and body in a pervasive and permanent way. I want to bring you to the place of complete wholeness I created you for. My healing work has already begun in your life—it began when I first drew you to myself. The deeper you go in me and the longer you abide in me, the more healing you will experience.

It is my healing touch that soothes your ailing body, your aching heart, your troubled mind, and your weary soul. It is my touch that heals you from the self-absorption that consumes you, the apathy toward me that depletes you, the lust that brings you shame and regret, the materialism that leaves you unsatisfied, the unforgiveness that isolates you from others—all the sin that has made your soul so sick.

Healer, touch me today as only you can . . .

My Comfort Goes on Forever

*Now may our Lord Jesus Christ himself and God our Father,
who loved us and by his grace gave us eternal comfort and a
wonderful hope, comfort you and strengthen you in every good
thing you do and say.* 2 Thessalonians 2:16-17

Do you find yourself longing for gentle comfort as you live
day to day in this rough-and-tumble world? My Spirit is the
Comforter. Come to me alone for the comfort you crave.

What is the comfort that I provide? It is the comfort of
confidence that your sin has been forgiven, the comfort of
knowing that you are accepted by me because of your union
with Christ, and the security of my solid commitment to save
you. Only in me can you enjoy the comfort of being bound
so securely to the risen and reigning Christ that you can face
death without fear, fully expecting to be raised with him to
reign with him.

*Oh, sweet Comforter, the comfort I find in you is not only
broad and vast, it is eternal. You are my only comfort in life
and death . . .*

I Will Take Revenge

Dear friends, never take revenge. Leave that to the righteous anger of God. For the Scriptures say, "I will take revenge; I will pay them back," says the LORD. Romans 12:19

When you are wronged, deep inside you pulses a demand for justice. And when you hear me instruct you never to take revenge, you may think that there will be no justice. But never think that entrusting wrongs to me means that those who hurt you will just get away with it. When you lay down the burden of vengeance, I will pick it up. This is not a subtle way of getting revenge, but it's giving vengeance to the one to whom it belongs.

In my universe, forgiveness does not mean that some crimes receive no punishment. It means that some crimes are punished in the suffering of a substitute. My wrath will repay every wrong—either in the suffering and death of Christ for those who repent and believe on him, or in hell for those who don't. You can trust me to be just.

I cannot continue to churn inside and dream of payback while my soul turns into acid. I will entrust this wrong to you. Your holy wrath is the only thing that can moderate my anger . . .

I Have Paid a Ransom to Save You

You know that God paid a ransom to save you from the empty life you inherited from your ancestors. And the ransom he paid was not mere gold or silver. It was the precious blood of Christ, the sinless, spotless Lamb of God. God chose him as your ransom long before the world began. 1 Peter 1:18-20

You were once captive, existing in a life devoid of meaning and purpose, going nowhere. But I paid a ransom to save you from that empty life. It wasn't with mere money that I paid your ransom but with the costly and precious blood of Christ. His blood is of infinite value, spilled on your behalf to free you from futility.

Because your ransom has been paid, you no longer are enslaved to the emptiness of materialism, the meaninglessness of ritualism, or the insidiousness of cynicism. I am filling up the emptiness in your life with good things—with myself. The blood of Christ is sufficient to free you from everything in your past that has bound you, and now you can freely enjoy the full life he has bought for you.

How can I ever thank you for paying the ransom that has set me free? You have filled the emptiness of my life with meaning and joy . . .

I Give Your Life Purpose and Meaning

*God said, "Let us make human beings in our image, to be like
us. They will reign over the fish in the sea, the birds in the sky,
the livestock, all the wild animals on the earth, and the small
animals that scurry along the ground."*   Genesis 1:26

I have blessed you with the highest honor I can bestow on any
creature, the greatest destiny I can call you to: you have been
made in my own image. Because you are as much like me as a
creature can be, your heart can love what I love and be broken
by that which breaks my own heart. You can begin to think
like me and bend your will toward mine.

And though my image in you was marred in the Fall, to
be my representative, reflecting me to the world, is your life's
greatest meaning. Perhaps you have seen this calling to reflect
my image as a burden, as one more thing you struggle with
and fail to live up to. But the more you simply abide in me
and share life with me, the more you'll look like me.

*Keep working in me, conforming me to your beautiful image,
making me all you intended me to be . . .*

My Law Will Set You Free

Don't just listen to God's word. You must do what it says. Otherwise, you are only fooling yourselves. . . . If you look carefully into the perfect law that sets you free, and if you do what it says and don't forget what you heard, then God will bless you for doing it. James 1:22, 25

How many years now have I been showering you with the goodness and guidance of my Word? Yet sometimes it does not seem to soak in. It is deflected by your disinterest, your distraction, your disobedience.

I am not pouring my truth into you to burden you or bore you. I want to bless you. So let my precepts sink into the soil of your life and nourish you. Linger over my Word. Turn the words and phrases over in your thoughts. Be bold enough and brave enough to do what the Scripture says, even when it is uncomfortable and inconvenient. Be pliable enough to bend your life to my law. I am not out to break you, but to bless you.

Sometimes your words are so familiar, I don't let them sink deep inside me. I foolishly doubt that they will quench the dryness of my soul. So rain down your Word on me and I will drink it in . . .

I Will Let You Gaze upon My Beauty

One thing I ask from the LORD, this only do I seek: that I may dwell in the house of the LORD all the days of my life, to gaze on the beauty of the LORD and to seek him in his temple.
Psalm 27:4, NIV

I made you with an inner longing for beauty. That's why it brings you such pleasure to see beauty in a lush green valley, a magnificent marble statue, or a perfect golf swing. Because of this longing for beauty, you can enjoy the loveliness of a piece of music, words well spoken, or an elegantly presented meal.

But all of these things are mere reflections of a far greater beauty. I am the ultimate beauty you were made to enjoy. Your longing for beauty is really a longing for me.

I am beautiful, and you will enjoy my beauty forever. What makes me beautiful is not just my individual attributes, but also their relationship to each other. When you see my beauty, you are beholding a perfect harmony and balance of my perfections. Now you see in part, but the day will come when you will see in full and will worship.

What a joy it is to know that I will spend eternity gazing upon your beauty that will not fade . . .

I Will Take You Home

*We are fully confident, and we would rather be away from these
earthly bodies, for then we will be at home with the Lord.*
2 Corinthians 5:8

The day is coming when your body will become a lifeless shell.
But this is not something to dread. It will be a welcome relief
from the difficulties and pain of life in a broken world. And
in that moment, your soul will enter immediately into my
presence. On that day, you will finally feel fully at home. No
more sense of unfulfilled longing. No more lonely waiting.

While your soul will be completely content in my presence, I will not leave you as a soul without a body forever.
I have something better in mind for your eternal future. Your
body will not be in the ground forever. I will raise it up and
remake it. It will be completely you but made radically new,
no longer vulnerable to disease or aging or injury. This divine
makeover will make you completely pleasing to me, and we
will live together in the new heaven and new earth.

*Lord, some days I just want to go home and be with you. And
other days, I love this life and the world and want to linger
here. I praise you for this blessed hope that whether I am here
or at home with you, I'm in your hands . . .*

I Have Set My Heart on You

The LORD did not set his heart on you and choose you because
you were more numerous than other nations, for you were the
smallest of all nations! Rather, it was simply that the LORD
loves you, and he was keeping the oath he had sworn to your
ancestors.   Deuteronomy 7:7-8

Just as I set my heart to love the people I chose and called
to myself long ago, so have I set my heart on you—to love
you, to be good to you, and to bring you into all that I have
planned for you. You didn't earn my love through your personal worthiness or good behavior, and you cannot lose my
love through your unworthiness or bad behavior. My love for
you is based on the covenant I made even when I knew you
could not live up to your part in it. But because you, my
beloved, are joined to Christ, you can be certain that my love
and commitment to you will not fade or fail.

Lord, I'm well aware of my unworthiness. So keep my gaze fixed
firmly on the complete worthiness of Christ. Through Christ I
get in on the blessings of your covenant love . . .

My Spirit Is Leading You to Life

Those who are dominated by the sinful nature think about sinful things, but those who are controlled by the Holy Spirit think about things that please the Spirit. So letting your sinful nature control your mind leads to death. But letting the Spirit control your mind leads to life and peace.   Romans 8:5-6

I know you are looking to me for life and peace, and this is exactly what I long to give you. But you must be aware that there is a battle for control going on in your mind. Your nature, apart from my Spirit, is always angling for the upper hand.

The kind of living I'm calling you to and empowering you for is not natural; it is supernatural. It is a work of the Holy Spirit in your life, by faith, on the basis of Christ's death and resurrection. I give my Holy Spirit to those who trust in Christ, and he brings about changes that could never and would never be made without him, so that he is glorified.

Holy Spirit, I'm giving you control of my mind today. I don't want to think about or do what comes naturally. Write your law on my heart so that I will value and desire what leads to life . . .

I Will Not Let You Ignore My Salvation

What makes us think we can escape if we ignore this great
salvation that was first announced by the Lord Jesus himself
and then delivered to us by those who heard him speak?
Hebrews 2:3

So much is coming at you all the time in this modern world,
and much of it you must simply ignore. So much noise, so
many demands are not worthy of your attention. But there
is one thing you must not ignore: your salvation. You cannot
take it for granted or give it no thought.

But I am not telling you to get to work so as to earn this
salvation. Rather, I'm reminding you not to ignore being
loved by me. Don't ignore being forgiven, accepted, protected,
strengthened, and guided by me. Don't ignore Christ's death
on the cross in your place. Don't ignore enjoying the free
access to my throne of grace. Don't ignore the inexhaustible
treasure of my promises. Claim the great salvation I hold out
to you as your own, and make it a part of your day-to-day life.
Live in the wonder of this great salvation.

The salvation you have given to me is not second-rate. It is
a great salvation. It is worthy of my attention, worthy of my
celebration, worthy of my glad proclamation . . .

I Am Cultivating Real Change in You

This same Good News that came to you is going out all over the world. It is bearing fruit everywhere by changing lives, just as it changed your lives from the day you first heard and understood the truth about God's wonderful grace.   Colossians 1:6

I have set up shop in your heart and gone to work. How will you know what I'm doing? You'll know when you find yourself being a friend to someone who needs one, when you are able to laugh even when things go against you, when you are at peace in the middle of chaos, when you are patient with someone who is difficult, when you are kind to someone who is unkind to you, when you do what is good and right even though what is bad and wrong sounds more interesting, when you follow through even though you're tired, and when you say no to your urge to do something you know you shouldn't. Enjoy me today as you discover I am changing you from the inside to become more like me.

Lord, I sense your Spirit is changing me on the inside. Please don't stop. Keep on changing me to be more like you . . .

I Have Given You a Privilege in Prayer

You can ask for anything in my name, and I will do it, so that the Son can bring glory to the Father. John 14:13

I have given you a special privilege that is reserved only for those who belong to me through Christ. You can ask me for anything in his name. It's not that "in Jesus' name" are magic words to be added to your prayers so that you will receive whatever you want. Adding "in Jesus' name" is not a secret formula for added effectiveness. Coming to me in the name of my Son means that you are asking for what you need on his authority and not your own, recognizing that Jesus is the one who has made it possible to approach me and expect to receive my grace. Coming to me in his name means that your requests are in line with his purposes for this world and for your life.

Having your prayers heard by me never depends on your use of certain formulas or required words but on your relationship with me—made possible by Christ's mediating work.

What a sacred privilege you've given me to bring my requests to you in Jesus' name. May I never dishonor his name by misusing it to seek after anything apart from your will . . .

I Bless You by Refusing to Be Diminished by You

He must become greater and greater, and I must become less and less. John 3:30

So many people in your world seek to define me in ways that diminish me and exalt themselves. But I will not let you diminish me with small thoughts of me. I cannot let you shrink me down into the smallness of an unexamined life. I will be big enough to you to disagree with you, make demands of you, and thrill you. I intend to flood your life with the abundant blessing of understanding all that I am for you in Christ Jesus. As you understand more and more what I have given to you in Jesus, your will will bend more easily, your ego will not demand so much stroking, and your heart will move more quickly to worship.

I am giving you the pleasure of admiring Someone greater than yourself. I am loving you by making you less preoccupied with yourself and your problems and more preoccupied with me and the greatness of my cause.

I have no interest in merely fitting you into my already full life and my firmly settled conclusions. I am putting away my small thoughts of you so that you can be to me as big as you really are. I'm giving you the final word in my life . . .

I Give You What You Need to Fight for Joy

Why am I discouraged?
    Why is my heart so sad?
I will put my hope in God!
    I will praise him again—
    my Savior and my God!   Psalm 42:5-6

When the dark clouds of discouragement and depression begin to gather in your life, sending you into a pit of despair, look up to me. I am extending to you a lifeline of solid hope. To take hold of this hope, you cannot merely listen to yourself but must challenge your desperate thoughts. Speak to yourself the truth about my goodness, my unfailing kindness, the rest I provide, and the acceptance I offer.

I'm not telling you to pretend that your life feels better than it really does, but I'm commanding you to look beyond your real disappointments to me, because I have enough joy for you too.

You can be overwhelmingly depressed and yet ruggedly hopeful. Look up and fight for joy as you let who I am go deep into your soul, reframing your desperate thoughts.

I cannot continue looking only downward and inward, finding no relief. I choose to look up and take hold of the hope found only in you . . .

I Will Show You What Path to Take

Trust in the LORD with all your heart; do not depend on your own understanding. Seek his will in all you do, and he will show you which path to take. Proverbs 3:5-6

Because you are my beloved child, I will never hide my will for you or delay in revealing it to you. You will find my perfect will for your life in my Word. As you meditate on my Word, it will reshape your values, reorder your priorities, and refine your character so that what I want for you will be clear.

My will for you and the path I want you to take is not so much about where you will go and what you will do as it is about who you will become and the relationship you will share with me. So keep on depending on me for what you need. Keep on turning to me for understanding. Keep on trusting me with the big things and the small things in your life. Then there will be no way you can miss the path I have set out for you.

Lord, I'm seeking your will. I want to walk in the path you have for me. And you are opening it before me, showing me what it means to walk in your way . . .

I Am Making You Truly and Eternally Rich

*People who long to be rich fall into temptation and are trapped
by many foolish and harmful desires that plunge them into ruin
and destruction.*   1 Timothy 6:9

An insatiable appetite for wealth will only make you miserable. I intend to save you from being endlessly unsatisfied,
irrelevant, selfish, and shallow. I'm calling you to find your
joy not in amassing more for yourself, but in giving more
away—in giving yourself away.

By no means am I suggesting that you impoverish yourself;
I'm showing you how to avoid impoverishing yourself. I'm
encouraging you to store up treasure in the only way you will
be able to enjoy it forever. I want you to be rich in good works,
generous and ready to share, and thereby store up heavenly
treasure for yourself. As you set your heart on me, confident
in my goodness, pouring out that confidence through a wealth
of good works serving others, you will accumulate that which
will enrich you forever.

*You are giving me everything freely through Christ. I don't
have to wear myself out with worry about whether I'll end up
impoverished. I can be calmly content, confident that you are
taking care of me as I give myself away . . .*

I Make My Will Clear to You

Let God transform you into a new person by changing the way you think. Then you will learn to know God's will for you.
Romans 12:2

Finding my will for your life is not like a game of hide-and-seek. You do not have to look for hidden clues to figure out what I want you to do. While I know the next specific step in your life, you will not find an instruction in my Word telling you to figure it out and follow it.

My broader will for your life has been made clear in my Word. And while it will take some effort on your part to understand and absorb my Word, my will is not hidden.

My Word does not tell you which person to marry or which profession to pursue or which town to live in. But as you saturate your mind in my revealed will, spelled out for you in the Bible, you will begin to think more like me, and you'll be better able to discern what I want for you.

So rather than asking me for some sort of special sign that will tell you what to do, continue asking me to renew your mind. Good students of my Word become wise decision-makers over a lifetime of following my clear instructions.

I see that my job is not to hunt for your secret will, but to do what you've clearly told me to do in your Word . . .

I Have Made Your Body into My Dwelling Place

Don't you realize that your body is the temple of the Holy Spirit, who lives in you and was given to you by God? You do not belong to yourself, for God bought you with a high price. So you must honor God with your body.   1 Corinthians 6:19-20

I bought you, paying the high price of the death of my beloved Son. I did not buy you to make you my slave, but to make you my dwelling place, to fill you with my very presence. Your body has now been set apart for my Holy Spirit to live in.

Just as the priests had to be pure to come into my dwelling place in the Temple, so must you keep my dwelling place pure. You cannot profane my temple with any sort of sexual immorality, treating your body as if it were yours to do with as you please. Instead, I want you know the joy of honoring me with your body. Honor me with how you engage your mind for my cause, with how you touch hurting people in my name, with where your feet take you to live out my gospel. I want you to use your body in ways that show the world that I am more satisfying, more precious, more to be desired than anything the body craves.

Purify this body of mine that is your temple, Lord. Let the words of my mouth and the meditations of my heart honor you . . .

I Have Set Aside a Day of Rest for You

Be careful to keep my Sabbath day, for the Sabbath is a sign of the covenant between me and you from generation to generation. It is given so you may know that I am the LORD, who makes you holy. . . . You have six days each week for your ordinary work, but the seventh day must be a Sabbath day of complete rest, a holy day dedicated to the LORD. Exodus 31:13, 15

You are so often busy and tired, and you so often feel the pressure of not enough time. So will you receive the gift of my rest? The lifestyle of rushing around from one activity to the next, trying to get ahead in life, always working and never waiting is not the abundant life I have for you. I'm calling you to stand against the strivings of the surrounding culture and honor me with one day in seven given over to worship and works of mercy.

People who think their lives consist of struggling to get more and more can never slow down because they won't ever have enough. But when you keep my Sabbath, you say to me and to the world around you that you trust me to provide everything you need with six days' worth of work.

The Sabbath is not an obligation you have placed on me for your benefit but a gift you have given to me for my blessing. So I will stop. I will rest . . .

I Am a Good Shepherd to You

The LORD is my shepherd; I have all that I need.   Psalm 23:1

I am not simply a shepherd to the world at large. I am your Shepherd. I know you. Indeed, I know you better than you know yourself. I know your past and your future, your secrets, your fears, your ambitions. This penetrating knowledge could be frightening to you were it not coupled with my care. But my perfect understanding of you is wedded to my perfect love for you.

So you can be confident that what I send you is what you need, and whatever you need, I will provide. And you can be content even if your ship never comes in, your dream never comes true, or the situation never changes. You have a God who hears you, the Holy Spirit within you, a Savior who keeps you, and the riches of heaven ahead of you. Because I am your Shepherd, you have grace for every sin, direction for every turn, an anchor for every storm. You have everything you need. And nothing can take it away from you.

I'm surrendering this cumbersome sack of discontent to you, Lord. I entrust myself to your care, believing that you are the fulfillment of all of my deep longings . . .

I Will Give You Grander Thoughts

Letting your sinful nature control your mind leads to death. But letting the Spirit control your mind leads to life and peace.
Romans 8:6

You have a mind-set and a viewpoint. You have attitudes and thought patterns that are deeply ingrained, and you are not predisposed to challenging them. But I am. I intend to show you your old ways of thinking—me first; if it feels good, do it; I deserve it; I am the master of my own destiny—and save you from them.

Not only do you think wrongly about yourself and about this world, you don't naturally think good and right thoughts about me. In fact, it is worse than that. On your own, your thoughts about me diminish and dishonor me. But I want to fill your mind with worthy thoughts of me.

I have given you a new filter to run all of your thoughts through—my Word. It will give you an eternal perspective that will reshape your value system, realign your priorities, and rework your personality. My Spirit will change how you think, what you want, and even how you feel.

Your Word has gotten me thinking new thoughts, seeing things from a new perspective, even feeling differently about things, and I love it . . .

I Will Assuage Your Anger toward Me

The people will declare, "The LORD is the source of all my righteousness and strength." And all who were angry with him will come to him and be ashamed. Isaiah 45:24

When I don't answer your prayer in the way you hoped I would, or when I allow what brings you pain, you may be tempted to become angry with me. It's natural to be angry when you don't get your way, and I am an easy target for that anger. In fact, many believers around you may encourage you to freely express it to me.

While you need never hide your true self from me, neither do you want to give free rein to your anger. Instead, turn to me for correction. I will correct whatever misunderstanding you've had about my purposes and promises that you think gives you grounds for your anger. Pour out your angry feelings before me—not in pride and accusation, but in humility and brokenness. As you inform your feelings by what you know to be true about me from my Word, you can reject the temptation to turn your back on me.

Lord, when my disappointment descends into anger toward you, I need you to correct my wrong assumptions and soothe my strong feelings. Give me your grace and your peace . . .

I Have Set Before You a Race to Run

Let us strip off every weight that slows us down, especially the sin that so easily trips us up. And let us run with endurance the race God has set before us. Hebrews 12:1

The life of faith is not a sprint but a marathon. You do not chart your own path but set your sights on the path I have set before you. And there is no doubt that you can finish the course I have marked out uniquely for you. I will equip you to do what I have called you to do. Some days you may sprint and other days you might plod, but you must continue to persevere.

To run your race well, you are going to have to strip away every weight that keeps you from making steady progress in drawing near to me. Lay down that load of legalism that keeps you bound up. Throw off that weight of unmet expectations and unnecessary activity. You will also need to turn away from every sin that repeatedly trips you up. You know what it is— that sin that seems to keep showing up. Turn to me and I will help you cut it away, put it to death, so that you can keep running in my direction.

Now that you've saved me, I cannot sit down and wait for heaven. I am running my race with an aim to finish well. Your Word is my fuel and your Spirit is the wind at my back . . .

I Will Not Abandon You to Your Own Intuition

"My thoughts are nothing like your thoughts," says the LORD.
"And my ways are far beyond anything you could imagine."
Isaiah 55:8

From the minute you awoke this morning, your mind has been filled with a stream of thoughts, an internal conversation with yourself. I must interrupt. I want to change the subject from your thoughts to my thoughts.

More than you realize, you operate out of unexamined gut reactions that deplete you rather than enrich you. Your natural thoughts reinforce your natural traits, tendencies, and opinions. This is why I've given you my very own Word and called you to saturate your mind in it. Through my Word, I give you wonderfully higher ways of thinking. I'm calling you to put all of your thoughts through the grid of my Word so that you can see everything in a new way, with my glory at the center. I will give you true insight and knowledge.

There is a grand canyon of separation between your thoughts and mine, between your ways and mine. As I take in your Word, think it through, talk about it, and meditate on it, teach me to think in new God-centered ways . . .

While You May Lose, You Will Not Lose Out

In his kindness God called you to share in his eternal glory by means of Christ Jesus. So after you have suffered a little while, he will restore, support, and strengthen you, and he will place you on a firm foundation. 1 Peter 5:10

Can you perceive my eternal glory that is ahead for you? I know it is sometimes difficult to see through the suffering that is so present with you today. But don't let today's troubles blind you to tomorrow's triumph. Just because you are losing much does not mean you will lose out.

After you've suffered a little while—and really this life is a little while in light of eternity—after you've gotten knocked around, put down, and overlooked in this life, I will restore you. You will not be damaged goods or carry psychological scars. You will be happy and whole with no regrets or backward glances. The day will never come when you will regret living all out for Christ, thinking it too costly. You'll be glad you stood firm, confident that everything you lost was worth it for all that you have gained.

I have set my sights not on my struggles and sorrows, but on your glory and grace . . .

My Commandments Are for Your Good

You must not have any other god but me. Exodus 20:3

I am calling you out of your world of scattered attachments into an exclusive, intimate relationship with me. This is how I want to bless you—to claim you as mine alone.

Our intimacy will thrive in exclusivity. We'll begin to share the closeness you've always longed for as you discover the pleasure of knowing me and being fully known by me. You will stop running to lesser saviors for comfort, and stop investing yourself in what brings no return for your soul.

The longer you tolerate rival gods lingering even on the fringes of your life, the more attached you become, and the more you push me into the background. So won't you sever those ties and make more room for my presence?

I am giving myself wholly to you with no reserve. And it is your whole heart, your whole life I am jealous to have as mine.

No other god deserves my heart or can satisfy my heart. You alone are my God. I will not share my heart with any other . . .

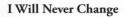

I Will Never Change

I am the LORD, and I do not change.   Malachi 3:6

Styles change, cultures change, governments change, people change. You change your mind, your preferences change, and your perspective changes.

But I do not change.

My gospel will never change; the good news that I save sinners will never become irrelevant. My plans for this world will not change; I will bring everything to its appointed end. My character will not change; you can always be sure that I will act in perfect righteousness and love. My power over the universe will not be diminished, and my love for my people will not grow cold. My Word will not change. It might be misquoted and misused, rejected and ridiculed, but it cannot be corrupted. It stands forever, certain and unchanging.

Humans are unreliable, unsteady, and inconsistent. Even good intentions come and go. But you have a God in the heavens who does not change.

You are a solid and secure foundation to build my life on when everything around me is shifting and uncertain. How good it is to know that you will never change your mind about me . . .

I Am Calling You to the Freedom of Confession

If we claim we have no sin, we are only fooling ourselves and not living in the truth. But if we confess our sins to him, he is faithful and just to forgive us our sins and to cleanse us from all wickedness.   1 John 1:8-9

I don't want you to live in the darkness, held hostage by hidden sin. Every sin that shames you can be washed away as it is brought into the light. So as I point out the sin that has come between us, instead of excusing it, confess it.

Sin shuns the light and wants to remain hidden. There, unexpressed, it poisons the whole person. But when the light of the gospel breaks into this dark seclusion of the heart, when the unexpressed is openly acknowledged, it loses its power. You are no longer alone with this evil but, through confession, you hand it over to me. As you come out of hiding, you stand in the fellowship of sinners who live by my grace—healed, forgiven, cleansed—with nothing to hide.

I hear you telling me that if I will conceal nothing, you will cleanse everything. I will not linger in the lonely darkness but will come into the light to be loved by you . . .

I Will Give You Everything You Need

Seek the Kingdom of God above all else, and live righteously, and he will give you everything you need.   Matthew 6:33

There are really two agendas you can pursue in life. One is to set out to secure a good job, comfort, predictability, and security, planning to add in spiritual things as you can. The other is to pursue a life that is pleasing to me, a life of giving yourself away for my cause, confident that I will throw in all of the other good stuff too.

Seeking is intentional; it's aggressive. It involves risk and boldness. Living this way is how you become untangled from the status quo. It's how you live in this world as a true citizen of the counterculture called the Kingdom of God.

As you make your budget or plan your schedule, something will come first. Do your budget and your schedule say "me first" or "Christ first"? Whatever you put first is what you really believe will take care of you. Trust me to take care of the lesser stuff so you can go after a higher cause.

I don't want to merely fit you into a life that I'm living for myself. I want to seek you first, knowing that you will give me everything I need for the life mission you have set for me . . .

I Give You Grace and Peace

May God give you more and more grace and peace.   1 Peter 1:2

I want to bless you today with multiplied grace and peace. Isn't it just what you need right now? Grace is my loving you without cause. While you love people whom you deem as deserving, I love for no reason—at least no reason within you. The reason is within me. Within me is all the incentive I need to love you. And I can love anyone into heaven—even you.

When you appropriate my grace, you are ready to experience my peace. My peace does not primarily consist of calm feelings and a serene outlook. Rather, it is an objective peace that is the result of being made right with me through the justifying work of Christ. Peace is the new condition grace creates—a new relationship with me, with others, and with your own conscience.

The more you know of me, the more familiar you are with my promises; the more your thinking is shaped and saturated by my Word, the more grace and peace will be multiplied to you.

I need more grace and peace today, Lord, to be accepted by you, empowered to live for you, at rest in you . . .

I Have Good Things Planned for You

*We are God's masterpiece. He has created us anew in Christ
Jesus, so we can do the good things he planned for us long ago.*
Ephesians 2:10

I know that sometimes you struggle with the way I have made
you—the shape or size of your body, your personality, the
abilities you were or weren't given. But these things do not
define you. These things do not determine your value or use-
fulness, and they cannot keep you from accomplishing the
purpose for which I made you.

You are my masterpiece. Your true beauty and value are
seen when you are used by me, your Master, to meet the needs
of the hurting world around you. The reason it feels so good
to offer food to someone who is hungry, a coat to someone
who is cold, friendship to someone who is lonely, or a home
to a child who is alone, is that this is what you were made for.
Your joy in these things is but a taste of my joy as I make your
life into a masterpiece that I can use.

*I recognize that you've made me as I am to use me in a unique
way. Forgive me for wasting so much time regretting how you've
made me. I want to celebrate the way you've created me and
how you're using me in this world . . .*

I Am Pruning You for Greater Fruitfulness

I am the true grapevine, and my Father is the gardener. He cuts off every branch of mine that doesn't produce fruit, and he prunes the branches that do bear fruit so they will produce even more.   John 15:1-2

As the master gardener, I know just how to nurture you into a fruitful branch in my vineyard. My strategy for coaxing a greater harvest from your life may not be what you would prefer. My plan is to prune—to reduce and cut away. I prune away commitments that will sap you of energy for investing in what will last forever. I sever relationships that are not nourishing your intimacy with me. I may cut out some of the activity you enjoy so that in the stillness you can hear my voice.

My pruning is not punishment; it is the answer to your prayers. It will save you from shortsighted desires and small ambitions that produce a lot of worthless growth. But pruning is cutting, and cutting hurts. Be assured that my pruning is never arbitrary, never reckless, never just to make a point. I am a master gardener. You can trust me to handle you carefully.

Though I flinch at the sound of your shears, Lord, do your pruning. Cut away anything and everything that keeps me from greater fruitfulness . . .

I Will Lead You into New-Covenant Rest

Christ has obtained a ministry that is as much more excellent than the old as the covenant he mediates is better, since it is enacted on better promises. For if that first covenant had been faultless, there would have been no occasion to look for a second. Hebrews 8:6-7, ESV

I am a God of covenant, and my covenants are good. My old covenant said, "Do this, and I will bless you; fail to do it, and I will curse you." The fault lay not with my covenant but with people's hearts. Obedience by willpower rather than through reliance on the Spirit simply doesn't work.

But my new covenant says, "You've broken my law beyond your capacity to fix it. So I've done everything for you through Christ. Enter into him and live in eternal security." In this way I overcome your rebellion and resistance, writing my will on your heart.

My old covenant helped you to come to the end of yourself—as you discovered that you do not have the power apart from me to obey. I have led you into new-covenant rest as you trust in Christ to do for you what you cannot do for yourself.

Everything you demand of me, you also provide for me freely and forever through Christ . . .

I Speak Grace and Truth to You

The law was given through Moses, but God's unfailing love and faithfulness came through Jesus Christ. John 1:17

Here is what you can count on in my dealings with you. I will tell you the truth—about myself, about this world, and about you—even when that truth is hard to hear. I have no interest in speaking false flattery that denies reality for politeness's sake. My Word cuts deep and reveals wrong. My Spirit brings conviction.

If I spoke only truth, you would have cause to become fearful, because we both know the truth about what is going on in your heart and in your mind. But you have no cause to fear, because the truth I speak to you is mingled with grace—grace that provides forgiveness for wrong and grace that provides power for change.

So open your Bible to hear me speak the truth to you. And open your life before me to experience my sufficient grace.

How I need you to speak truth to me, Lord. But I can bear it only because you also speak grace. I need them both, so shower me with your truth and grace . . .

I Have Given You a Sacred Longing

We know that all creation has been groaning as in the pains of childbirth right up to the present time. And we believers also groan, even though we have the Holy Spirit within us as a foretaste of future glory, for we long for our bodies to be released from sin and suffering.   Romans 8:22-23

I know that you sometimes groan inwardly over the pain and suffering and sadness in the world. You ache over all of the hurt even as you wait for me to make it all new. You wonder why I wait, why I do not come now and put an end to the pain. But I assure you that the day will come when the groaning and anticipation will be over. You will say that it was worth the wait, that enjoying my presence in the perfection of a redeemed creation was worth waiting for.

Don't think that something is deficient in your faith when you can't share in the happy-all-the-time religion of some. When you find yourself groaning because of the death and destruction, the disease and deprivation in this world, and you find deep inside an intense longing for all of it to be erased and made right, that is a sacred longing, placed deep within you by my Spirit.

I am longing for the day you will set everything right in this world. Come quickly, Lord Jesus . . .

I Have Shined My Light into Your Dark Heart

God, who said, "Let there be light in the darkness," has made this light shine in our hearts so we could know the glory of God that is seen in the face of Jesus Christ. 2 Corinthians 4:6

Many people think they are smart enough, strong enough, or savvy enough to come to me. But you know better. You know that I am the One who revealed myself to you, who drew you to myself and made you new. It is not something that you figured out on your own.

The truth is, you were in the darkness of your sin, not even looking for me, and I made my light shine into the darkest recesses of your heart. Just as the mere revelation of my will in saying "Let there be" at Creation brought all that exists out of nothing, so has my divine decree brought spiritual life out of the deadness in your heart.

I have turned my face toward you in Jesus Christ. There is no place in your heart for pride, only joy and gratitude.

Forgive me, Lord, for my arrogance in sometimes thinking I am better or smarter than someone else because I belong to you. It's all you . . .

It Is My Pleasure to Give You the Kingdom

Don't be concerned about what to eat and what to drink. Don't worry about such things. . . . Seek the Kingdom of God above all else, and he will give you everything you need. So don't be afraid, little flock. For it gives your Father great happiness to give you the Kingdom.   Luke 12:29, 31-32

Your worry is useless. It projects the worst and loads the present with the weight of the future. So let it go. Refuse to keep feeding it with your thoughts. Instead, crowd out those anxious thoughts with a greater concern, a more fruitful endeavor. Pour your energy into bringing even more of your life under my authority and care. Invest your concern not in getting your own needs met (I know what you need and I will take care of you), but in meeting the needs of the world around you.

As you obsess less about food, clothing, and the essentials you need for life, and as you give more of yourself over to me, you'll find yourself liberated from anxiety.

How wonderful it is to know that you find great happiness in giving yourself to me and extending your loving rule in my life . . .

I Will Give You a Heart to Forgive

Be kind to each other, tenderhearted, forgiving one another, just as God through Christ has forgiven you. Ephesians 4:32

I know you don't have it in yourself to forgive, but my Holy Spirit in you can give you what you need. I began this good work in you as I granted to you great forgiveness, and I will be faithful to complete it as my forgiveness overflows in your life toward those who hurt you.

I am at work creating a tender heart for forgiveness in place of that old hard heart of yours. As you welcome him to work, my Spirit is generating fruit in the interior of your life—loving actions in place of hateful thoughts, joyful interactions in place of uncomfortable avoidance, peaceful thoughts in place of inner turmoil, patience in place of anger, kindness in place of coldness, goodness in place of payback, gentle responses in place of harsh words, faithful endurance in place of walking away, and self-control in place of surrendering to what comes naturally.

This resentment really isn't worth holding on to. I want to grab hold of a life that is so full of gratitude for being forgiven, that forgiveness will spill out on everyone around me . . .

I Will Satisfy Your Longing

God blesses those who hunger and thirst for justice, for they will be satisfied.   Matthew 5:6

You long for the world to be set right—to be awash in a righteousness not its own. You long for the world to be a place where there is peace with God and one another—no tense marriages, no racial hatred, no false worship, nothing but normal life overflowing with fullness in Christ. Your heart is set on a perfected universe enjoyed by perfected human beings under Christ the King of Grace.

This healthy hunger—this holy hunger—is evidence of my blessing in your life. The triumph of my grace in you is not your avoidance of sin but your hunger and thirst for righteousness. Your eager appetite proves that you will be satisfied.

Don't be ashamed of your unfulfilled desires; they are the best part of you. Bring them with you as you come to me. Don't grow weary in waiting for satisfaction. The rightness I bring and the justice I will accomplish are the feast you were made for.

Lord, I'm hungry and thirsty. I see that you are offering me infinite satisfaction as I set my heart on the solid joys and lasting treasures of your Kingdom . . .

I Am Shaping Your Life

LORD, you are our Father. We are the clay, and you are the potter. We all are formed by your hand. Isaiah 64:8

You are in my hands, being shaped and formed just as a potter shapes clay. The difficulties you face bring you against the pressure of the potter's wheel, and my sovereign hand holds you there. You can resist my shaping through rebellion or resentment. You can become offended with me and determine to form your life into your image of what is worthwhile and beautiful. Or you can welcome my work and allow me to mold your life into something of great worth and beauty.

I know that you don't always appreciate the way I'm shaping your life. You wonder why I have made you the way you are or why I am not using you in the place you desire. But know that I am molding you according to my own wise purpose. You can trust me to shape your life into a vessel of honor that is fit for displaying my own great glory.

I give you this lump of clay called my life, Lord. Use whatever pressure is needed to shape me into something of great worth in your sight, something of beauty in your estimation, something fit for displaying your glory . . .

My Name Is a Safe Refuge

The name of the LORD is a strong fortress; the godly run to him and are safe.   Proverbs 18:10

My names tell you something special about who I am and how I want to give myself to you. When you are in need and my resources are at hand, I am Yahweh-Yireh: the Lord provides. When you are sick and I bring relief, I am Yahweh-Rophi: the Lord who heals. When you find yourself in a spiritual battle and I give you victory, I am Yahweh-Nissi: the Lord our banner. When I give you a desire for holiness, I am Yahweh-M'Kaddesh: the Lord who sanctifies. When your anxiety is overcome by my peace, I am Yahweh-Shalom: the Lord is peace. When I give you victory over any evil that threatens you, I am Yahweh-Sabaoth: the Lord of hosts. When I lovingly bring you back into the fold from your wanderings, I am Yahweh-Rohi: the Lord my shepherd. When you accept the sinless perfection of Christ in place of your own sinfulness, I am Yahweh-Tsidkenu: the Lord our righteousness. When you feel lonely and find me reaching out to you, I am Yahweh-Shammah: the Lord who is there.

Everything I need I find in your name . . .

I Have Reconciled You to Myself

He has reconciled you to himself through the death of Christ in his physical body. As a result, he has brought you into his own presence, and you are holy and blameless as you stand before him without a single fault.   Colossians 1:22

There was once a time when we were alienated and estranged. Your mind was hostile toward me. We were enemies. Something had to be done to bring reconciliation—something costly. But it was not you who paid the cost so that we might be reconciled. I paid it through the death of Christ, and now we have peace.

So when you wake up in the morning, there is no need to dread the day. When you head out the door, there is no need to fear what could happen. When you lay your head down at night, you can drift into sleep knowing that if you should not awake again in this world, you will awake in my presence. And there will be no cause for fear in facing me because every sin you have ever committed and ever will commit is forgiven, and we have been fully reconciled.

You have saved me from being alienated and hostile and have made me holy, blameless, and faultless. You have brought me into your presence, and I have no cause for fear . . .

I'm Inviting You to Share in the Disgrace of Jesus

Jesus suffered and died outside the city gates to make his people holy by means of his own blood. So let us go out to him, outside the camp, and bear the disgrace he bore. Hebrews 13:12-13

I know that you have a desire for significance and acceptance—that you were hoping to turn heads with your beauty and brilliance. But I also know that you want what is real and lasting. And so I must tell you that real satisfaction is to be found in sharing the disgrace of Jesus on the cross—like a common criminal on the outskirts of town.

I am calling you to a life of rejection because of your identification with Christ, a life of being an outsider when you love to be accepted and welcomed as an insider. I am calling you to share, not in the applause, but in the reproach of Jesus.

But that is just for now. I am asking you to trade in acceptance in the here and now, the city of this world, for the welcome you will receive in the city I am preparing, the city of God. When you walk into that city, nothing you have given up will seem like a sacrifice. It will have been worth it.

Jesus, I believe that being welcomed by you on that day will be worth being rejected by the world here and now. So I come to you . . .

I Am Teaching You to Rely on Me, Not Yourself

We were crushed and overwhelmed beyond our ability to endure, and we thought we would never live through it. In fact, we expected to die. But as a result, we stopped relying on ourselves and learned to rely only on God, who raises the dead.
2 Corinthians 1:8-9

People may tell you that I will never give you more than you can handle. But don't listen; it's not true. You will often find yourself in situations that require more faith, more perseverance, more love, and more wisdom than you have on your own. And when you find yourself in this situation you will realize how much you need me. In fact, you'll be desperate for me. The truth is, you were just as desperate for me before you found yourself in this place; you just didn't realize it. Sometimes you need to be shaken so that you can see your sin of self-reliance. Then you can repent of this sin and become more God-reliant.

It is not a sign of weakness to depend on me. It is a sign of spiritual strength to live, day by day, in recognition of your utter dependence on me.

While I, and the culture around me, value independence, I realize now that you value dependence. Forgive me, Lord, for my stubborn self-reliance. I'm turning to you. I can't do it on my own . . .

I Will Elevate You to a Place of Great Honor

He gave up his divine privileges;
*   he took the humble position of a slave*
*   and was born as a human being.*
When he appeared in human form,
*   he humbled himself in obedience to God*
*   and died a criminal's death on a cross.*
Philippians 2:7-8

The pattern for Christ was this: humility before honor, suffering before glory, descending to lowliness before being exalted to the highest place. Does it not make sense that I intend for your life to be patterned after his? Understanding this will enable you to endure the humbling hardships of this life. You will be able to persevere knowing that just as the suffering of Jesus resulted in his exaltation to a place of great honor, so will your suffering for my sake result in your future exaltation to a place of great honor in my eternal kingdom.

You can be certain that after humility, there is honor. After the cross comes a crown.

While I lift myself up, the Son of God stepped down. While I make a big deal of myself, Jesus made himself nothing. While I measure out my obedience one inch at a time to keep control, Jesus became obedient to the point of death. So develop in me the same attitude that Jesus had . . .

My Word Is Exposing What Needs to Be Cut Away

The word of God is alive and powerful. It is sharper than the sharpest two-edged sword, cutting between soul and spirit, between joint and marrow. It exposes our innermost thoughts and desires. Hebrews 4:12

My Word throws on the light in the dark places of your life, revealing the sin that has made itself at home. My Word cuts deeply, laying bare the ugliness in your character that you might wish to keep hidden. And while this cutting may be painful, you can be confident that it is purposeful. I am cutting away what displeases me.

I know that you do not relish the idea of having your inner life exposed, your thought life and motives laid bare. But you are unable to hide anything from my penetrating gaze, and you are better for the exposure. You do not need to be afraid. As I expose your shallow beliefs and false intentions with the truth of my Word, you will no longer have to live with an overwhelming sense of hypocrisy. The faith you claim will become an increasing reality in the way you live.

I am opening myself up to your Word, Lord. Transform my inner ugliness so that I radiate your beauty. Cut away anything and everything that keeps me from bearing your likeness . . .

I Will Not Be Fair; I Will Show Mercy

Have mercy on me, O God, because of your unfailing love.
Because of your great compassion, blot out the stain of my sins.
Psalm 51:1

Whenever you experience hardship or difficulty, you are quick to say, "I don't deserve this!" You believe you have a right to fairness and feel violated when you haven't gotten what you think you deserve. On the surface, a perfectly fair world appeals to you. But in a completely fair world, there would be no room for grace—receiving what you don't deserve. There would be no room for mercy, either—being spared from getting the punishment you rightly deserve. While you deserve punishment, you've received forgiveness; and while you deserve my judgment, you've experienced my love. While you deserve death, you are receiving unending, unstoppable life.

Living in the world, where you don't always get what you deserve and where you sometimes get what you don't deserve, means that sometimes you'll experience loss. But it also means that you can receive mercy.

If I got what was fair, what I really deserve, I would have to pay for my sin. But you have exacted your righteous judgment on an innocent substitute—Christ—and shown me mercy . . .

My Spirit Will Tell You the Truth

When the Spirit of truth comes, he will guide you into all truth. He will not speak on his own but will tell you what he has heard. He will tell you about the future. He will bring me glory by telling you whatever he receives from me. John 16:13-14

You need never fear that I am manipulating you or deceiving you. I always tell you the truth that you most need to hear. You are wise to judge all other voices by their harmony with mine.

My Holy Spirit is the One who helps you hear my voice and understand it. He is the Counselor, showing you what is true and what is false so that you can embrace the truth of who I am and what I'm offering to you. He is the Advocate, turning the words on the pages of your Bible into something powerful and personal that can penetrate your soul and change your heart. He is the Comforter, soothing your troubled heart with whispers of my love for you. Tune your ears to hear my Spirit speaking to you, and let the truth give you courage and peace.

Spirit, keep speaking the truth to me as I live in this world surrounded by false prophets and false teaching. Tell me the truth about myself. Tell me the truth about God's promises. Tell me the truth about all that is to come . . .

I Am Worthy of Your Trust in the Worst Times

Even though the fig trees have no blossoms, and there are no grapes on the vines; even though the olive crop fails, and the fields lie empty and barren; even though the flocks die in the fields, and the cattle barns are empty, yet I will rejoice in the LORD! I will be joyful in the God of my salvation!
Habakkuk 3:17-18

My great blessing to you is not that I will always save you from disaster. Sometimes you will experience the worst this broken world has to offer. My great blessing to you is that no matter what happens, even when the worst happens, you have the knowledge and confidence that you belong to a God who can be trusted with even this. Even though you don't know what I'm doing, you can believe that I know what I'm doing. Even though you may not understand how anything good can come out of what you're experiencing, you can believe that I understand how I am using all of this for your good.

Out of the greatest tragedy of all time—the death of Christ on the cross—you brought about the greatest good of all time: the salvation of sinners. So I can believe you will accomplish something good in what seems tragic in my life . . .

I Saw You Before You Were Born

You saw me before I was born. Every day of my life was
recorded in your book. Every moment was laid out before a
single day had passed. How precious are your thoughts about
me, O God. Psalm 139:16-17

Since before the day you were born, you have been in my heart
and on my mind. Without taking away your freedom, I have
been laying out my plans for your life. You see, your life is not
made up of random happenstance.

Take comfort in knowing that my plans for your life are
specific and complete. You don't have to be filled with fear
about the future or regret over the past. Nothing can happen
to you that is outside of my sovereign oversight. My plans for
your life are for your ultimate good, even when they don't
seem that way on the surface.

When life seems good, it is easy for me to celebrate that every
day of my life was recorded in your book. But when tragedy
strikes, on the days when my life is changed forever by loss,
I cannot help but wonder if this day was written in your book,
by your hand. I wonder if this is the story you intended to write
for my life or if there has been a terrible mistake. So help me to
rest in your loving thoughts toward me and my confidence that
you will do what is right . . .

I Have Made You Durable

We are pressed on every side by troubles, but we are not crushed. We are perplexed, but not driven to despair. We are hunted down, but never abandoned by God. We get knocked down, but we are not destroyed. Through suffering, our bodies continue to share in the death of Jesus so that the life of Jesus may also be seen in our bodies.   2 Corinthians 4:8-10

If this life is all you have, panic easily sets in when that life is threatened. If the world's wealth is all you anticipate you will inherit, then financial setbacks lay you low. And if it is up to you to make something of yourself, and you are going nowhere fast, there is cause for despair.

But you know this life is not all there is. You know that an imperishable inheritance awaits you in heaven, and that because you are connected to Christ your life has ultimate dignity and purpose. So you can face sickness, setbacks, and insults and not be done in. There is a rugged durability in the interior of your life, and as a result, your joy is not so fleeting and your confidence is not so easily shaken.

To be at the end of my resources is not to be at the end of your resources. Instead, being dependent on you positions me to experience your power breaking through my human dilemma . . .

I Am Your Comfort in Your Greatest Sorrow

God blesses those who mourn, for they will be comforted.
Matthew 5:4

One of the most beautiful evidences that you are living under my gracious blessing is your deep sadness over your sin. Though you know you're forgiven, you don't take sin lightly. I have given you eyes to see its insult to my grace, its offense before my holiness. And so, when your eyes are opened to your empty religiosity, your hidden motives, and your veiled pride, you have no desire to sweep your sin under the rug or explain it away. You see it through my eyes and rightfully mourn.

But you do not mourn forever. Your mourning is infused with hope and light. Into the darkness of your mourning floods the light of my abundant forgiveness, and you are comforted. While you feel the full weight of your sin and are sad, your confidence that I have borne this weight and carried it away breaks through your sadness in a burst of thanksgiving and joy.

You are blessing me, Lord, with a sadness that will make me happy forever. I will not rush through this redemptive sadness too quickly to peace, but to peace I will come . . .

Now You Can Enjoy Me without Fear

God . . . brought us back to himself through Christ. And
God has given us this task of reconciling people to him.
2 Corinthians 5:18

I have blessed you by making it possible for you to be close
to me. Jesus, by his death, has taken away all of the sin that
came between us by taking the punishment for it himself on
the cross. So now you can enjoy me without fear and discover
how good I really am. And as you enjoy me, I want you to
share your joy in me with those around you who have not
received this gift of acceptance through Jesus. This is not a
burden I am placing on you, but an invitation to share in the
joy I find when more and more people live in relationship
with me freely and forever. As you show others the way into
relationship with me, you'll discover what a blessing it is to
have another brother or sister in Christ beside you.

Thank you for bringing me back to yourself when I was far
away from you. Show me someone today who doesn't know
the joy I have from being in relationship with you . . .

I Will Welcome You

We can boldly enter heaven's Most Holy Place because of the blood of Jesus. By his death, Jesus opened a new and life-giving way through the curtain into the Most Holy Place.
Hebrews 10:19-20

You need never fear that the door into my presence will be slammed shut to you. Instead, I am throwing it wide open, welcoming you in, wanting you to come close.

You can come to me confidently and boldly—not confident in your own goodness or with a boldness that comes from arrogance or ignorance, but confident because you are in Christ. You're bold because you fully believe that his death has sufficiently paid for your sin and his blood has sufficiently cleansed you of sin.

Don't let anything or anyone keep you from drawing near to me. The essence and the joy of life in Christ is coming into my holy presence—not because I have lowered my standards or because you are deserving, but because Christ has opened the way for you.

Jesus, your flesh was torn so that a way could be opened for me to approach a holy God. This generous invitation comes to me at your great cost, and I will be thanking you throughout all eternity . . .

I Have Put My Glory at the Center

They were calling out to each other, "Holy, holy, holy is the LORD of Heaven's Armies! The whole earth is filled with his glory!" Isaiah 6:3

I have given you eyes to see my own overflowing abundance, which is gaining for me a reputation for being the most wonderful Person in the universe. This is what I created you to see and enjoy and reflect. I did not create you to make up for any lack in myself, but so that I would be more greatly glorified. I did not create you to make you the center of things, but so that you can enjoy making me the center of all things. In me, the most glorious Person imaginable reigns supreme in your joys and sorrows, in your failures and successes, moment by moment.

Most people spend their lives on a quest for their own glory, fighting for bragging rights—but not you. Because you have seen my glory, you have forsaken your own self-centeredness, confident that living for my glory not only honors me, it blesses you.

Lord, my life is not about me and my needs, my agendas, or my feelings, but about your glory filling this earth . . .

I Have Registered Your Name in Heaven

Don't rejoice because evil spirits obey you; rejoice because your names are registered in heaven.   Luke 10:20

There are many places where people are pleased to see their names—on an award plaque, a building, the team roster, a book cover, a diploma. But I have written your name in a place far more precious and infinitely longer lasting. I have written your name in my Book of Life, and it cannot be erased.

In fact, every day of your life was written in my Book before even one of them came to be. I have recorded your name as foreknown, predestined, conformed to the image of my Son, called, justified, glorified. You are loved, chosen, without fault, adopted, mine forever.

So you need not worry about your name going down in any history books or seeing your name in lights on some marquee. You need not become exhausted making a great name for yourself in this world. Your name is written where it really matters—in heaven—forever identifying you as belonging to me.

Nothing could give me greater or more lasting happiness and security than knowing my name is written in your Book . . .

I Have Made You Alive

*Once you were dead because of your disobedience and your
many sins. . . . But God is so rich in mercy, and he loved us
so much, that even though we were dead because of our sins,
he gave us life when he raised Christ from the dead.*
Ephesians 2:1, 4-5

Though you were born physically alive, you were spiritually
dead, with no inclination even to look for me. Don't fool
yourself into thinking that you were just a little bit sick with
sin, or in need of only a bit of inspiration to get going on the
right track. The worst news of your life is, "Once you were
dead." But that is not the end of your story, because the best
news of your life is, "But God . . ."

You had no power to say no to the sin that depleted you—
"But God . . ." You had no promise of anything good in your
future—"But God . . ." You had no place of safety from the
divine wrath you fully deserved—"But God . . ."

I walked by your open grave, and instead of turning away
from the stench, I called you to new life in my Son.

*The best two words I'll ever hear are surely, "But God . . ."
I was dead and you have given me life . . .*

I Will Lead You into the Joy of Surrender

He went on a little farther and bowed with his face to the ground, praying, "My Father! If it is possible, let this cup of suffering be taken away from me. Yet I want your will to be done, not mine." Matthew 26:39

Some people suggest that strong faith is defined by throwing your energies into begging me for a miracle that will take away your suffering and then believing without doubting that I will do it. But faith is not measured by your ability to manipulate me to get what you want, but rather by your willingness to submit to what I want.

What you need most is not to hear me say yes to your requests. What you need is to be filled with such deep confidence in the character of your Father that when I say no to you, you know I am doing what is right and good for you. What you need most is the faith to trust me.

As you bring your wants and pour them out before your Father, I will give you the courage you need to surrender, so you can say along with Jesus, "I want your will to be done, not mine."

I'm beginning to truly believe that the joy of surrendering to your will is going to be worth whatever it may cost me . . .

I Will Be Found by You

"In those days when you pray, I will listen. If you look for me wholeheartedly, you will find me. I will be found by you," says the LORD. Jeremiah 29:12-14

I am not a God who sets up hoops you must jump through or mystical mazes you must navigate to come into my presence. I have thrown the door wide open to you through prayer. You can be assured that when you quiet all of the noise in your life, and when you humble yourself before me, I will listen. I will glory in your praise and thanksgiving. I will hear your confession and forgive. I will consider your petition. And if you will not only speak to me but also listen for me, you will hear my voice speaking through my Word. Nothing matters more than my making myself known in your experience. This is how I will be glorified—as you experience wave after wave of the radiance of my very nature.

When you search for me, you will find me to be true to myself—a God of steadfast love, great goodness, and compassion. You'll wonder how you could ever have been foolish enough to resist me.

Lord, though my heart is so often divided, how I long to look for you wholeheartedly and find you in the quiet place . . .

I Will Refresh You

For I will pour out water to quench your thirst
*   and to irrigate your parched fields.*
And I will pour out my Spirit on your descendants,
*   and my blessing on your children.*   Isaiah 44:3

Have all of the demands and disappointments of day-to-day life in this world left you dry? Do you find yourself dreaming of going on vacation, taking a break, getting away? You do not have to change your location to find the refreshment you are longing for—only your orientation. Rather than running off, you need only look up. Rather than escape from your circumstances, what you need is refreshment in the midst of your circumstances. You need more of me, more of my Spirit showering you with the goodness of Christ.

My purpose in your life is not just to forgive your sins but also to give you more and more of myself. I refresh burned-out people with vitality from above. How? I pour freshness and vigor and hope into the desert places in your life—not a trickle of blessing but a downpour.

Flood my life with your Spirit, Lord. Make real to me all that Christ is worth by translating the doctrines of the gospel into an overflowing, nourishing, renewing experience of the heart . . .

I Have Called You into My Church

Christ loved the church. He gave up his life for her to make
her holy and clean, washed by the cleansing of God's word.
Ephesians 5:25-26

I love my church—the people I have called to myself from all
the peoples of the earth, the people I intend to call my own
for eternity. While I love you and care for you as an individual,
my grand plans for the future center on my church. I have
made my loyalty clear. And you find your home in me as you
find your place in the object of my affection: my church.

You will never discover all of the blessing I've reserved for
you if you take a privatized, consumerist, low-commitment
approach to the people closest to my heart. You cannot love
me fully if you do not also embrace what is most precious to
me—my church. I have not brought you to myself to send
you through this life alone. I want to bless you by using you,
as an essential part of my body, to bless the world.

Sometimes I find it inconvenient, costly, or even hurtful to give
myself to your beloved church, Lord. But I know you are not
only using the church to love me, you are using me to love the
world through your church . . .

I Have Given You Someone to Follow

Anyone who wants to be my disciple must follow me, because my servants must be where I am. And the Father will honor anyone who serves me.   John 12:26

When Christ said, "Follow me," he was not merely offering an invitation but issuing a command. Following him cannot be a halfhearted pursuit. If anything is keeping you from following Christ, you must get rid of it.

Following Christ will require that you stop following the ways of this world. He will lead you away from a life of chasing after possessions, experiences, and passions that will never ultimately satisfy you. Following Christ will save you from the tyranny of always thinking about yourself first—your needs, your discomforts, your hurts, your wants, your preferences, your rights. Instead, he will show you how to surrender your demands for the life you think you deserve so you'll want, most of all, to please me.

Follow Christ, not into a life of comfort, but into a life of significance. In the process, your life will witness to the world that you treasure him more than everything you relinquish in order to go after him.

I hear your voice calling and I am following after you, keeping my eye on you, conforming to you . . .

I Have Made You a Steward of My Good Gifts

The master said, "Well done, my good and faithful servant. You have been faithful in handling this small amount, so now I will give you many more responsibilities. Let's celebrate together!"
Matthew 25:23

Everything you have, I have given to you—everything you are and everything you enjoy, including your intelligence, your athletic ability, your social skills, your financial resources, and your unique talents. But I have not given it all to you to do with as you please. I've entrusted it to you to invest for a return for my Kingdom. I want to bless you by making you into a faithful steward of all of my good gifts to you.

What is it I have placed in your hands? Do you have undedicated time? Use it for me; don't waste it on things with no lasting value. Do you have relational insight? Use it to bless my people. Do you have entrepreneurial instincts? Build a business that builds my Kingdom. Do you have a platform? Use it to give out my gospel. Steward my good gifts well and I will give you even more.

How I long to hear the words "Well done" when I stand before you one day. Give me fresh insight for how I can use what you've given to me to make a difference in this world for you . . .

I Want to Rid Your Life of Something Rotten

You must all be quick to listen, slow to speak, and slow to get angry. Human anger does not produce the righteousness God desires. James 1:19-20

Living your life as a sinner among sinners, there will be plenty of times when someone rubs you the wrong way or significantly injures you, stirring up fiery feelings of anger. But then you have a choice about what you will do with those feelings. Will you replay those hurts again and again in your head, imagining how delicious it would be to put that person in his or her place? Or will you refuse to allow the poison of anger to rot you on the inside?

When someone hurts you, you will be tempted to be consumed by anger. But you don't have to give in to that temptation. While anger may be a natural reaction and even justifiable, I am all about transforming you on the inside so that you are no longer bound to do what comes naturally. My Spirit inside you will empower you to respond supernaturally. He will give you what you need so that you can stop demanding what you think you deserve from other people.

I don't want to be an angry person, always out for my pound of flesh. So Spirit, do your work in me. Put out the fire of my anger so I can let it go . . .

I Am Preparing a Place for You

Don't let your hearts be troubled. Trust in God, and trust also in me. There is more than enough room in my Father's home. If this were not so, would I have told you that I am going to prepare a place for you? John 14:1-2

I hear the longing in your heart for security and safety. Don't be surprised by hardship, and don't let your heart be troubled by it. Trust me to look out for you, protect you, provide for you. You can find real peace and lasting security only as you find your home in me.

Find comfort in the truth that I am preparing a place where you will forever be safe and secure with me. There will be no storms, no threats, and no fear—only perfect peace and safety.

This sure hope is a strong and trustworthy anchor for your soul when the winds of difficulty are blowing in your life. It is a promise you can depend on. Take hold of it, and then live and die like you believe it.

Every time I am tempted to fear, I remember that you are taking care of me. I will not leave this life and emerge into nothingness but into your loving presence. I can live and die in peace . . .

I Am Always Waiting to Welcome You Home

He returned home to his father. And while he was still a long way off, his father saw him coming. Filled with love and compassion, he ran to his son, embraced him, and kissed him.
Luke 15:20

What is the mental picture you have of me? Do you see me as a no-nonsense judge, a benevolent grandpa, a boring teacher, or an impossible-to-please boss? I want you to see me on my terms, as I truly am—a loving Father, filled with love and compassion for you, my child.

Even when you run away from me, ignoring me and wasting the resources I provide for you, I am still loving you and preparing to welcome you home. I'm not preparing a harsh lecture; I'm planning a lavish party.

So if the day ever comes when you wake up and realize that you've made a terrible mess of things and think that you've failed so miserably that you can't face me, let alone expect my forgiveness, remember this picture of me—waiting and watching, arms wide open, hurrying out to meet you—and come running in my direction.

What a loving Father you are that you would run in my direction even though I am not worthy to be called your child . . .

My Mercy Flows to the Worst of Sinners

The LORD said, "I will cause all my goodness to pass in front of you, and I will proclaim my name, the LORD, in your presence. I will have mercy on whom I will have mercy, and I will have compassion on whom I will have compassion."
Exodus 33:19, NIV

I love you for no reason—at least for no reason within you. The reason I love you is entirely within me. I am good to bad people for no reason except to be true to myself. My heart grows warm toward helpless people just to be true to myself. I decide who I'm going to love, and I love them endlessly forever. I am a self-motivated lover of people who deserve to be damned.

This means that the rottenness of your past is not an insurmountable obstacle to my gracious work in your life. In fact, I love to magnify the generosity of my grace by saving the worst of sinners. The outflow of my mercy to you is not a result of your decision but mine. When you chose me, it was because I had first chosen you.

Lord, I am not good enough to deserve your mercy, but neither am I too evil to be excluded from it. In fact it really isn't about me, but you. I stand in awe of your sovereign freedom to extend mercy on those you choose, and I worship with gratitude . . .

I Am Making You into a Temple Where I Will Dwell

You are coming to Christ, who is the living cornerstone of God's temple. He was rejected by people, but he was chosen by God for great honor. And you are living stones that God is building into his spiritual temple.   1 Peter 2:4-5

You are my special building project. I am taking you as you are—flawed and unfaithful—and making you fit for your place in my architectural plan. What makes you fit is your ongoing contact with the life-giving Cornerstone: Christ.

This is not something that happens because you go to church, but only because you come to Christ. This is not about becoming a church member, but about being adopted into my family.

As you continue in fellowship with Christ and with all who come to him, you are the heart and center of my activity in the world. You are being built up into a residence intended for my very presence.

Lord, I have no need of finding some sacred space to get close to you. Indeed, you have made your home within me. Spirit, shape me into a living stone that will bring you great honor . . .

I Am the God You Need

Those who wish to boast should boast in this alone: that they truly know me and understand that I am the LORD who demonstrates unfailing love and who brings justice and righteousness to the earth, and that I delight in these things.
Jeremiah 9:24

Plenty of people think they have no need for me. But you know better. I have blessed you with a profound understanding of who I am and how I am meeting your greatest needs.

I demonstrate unfailing love—the kind of sturdy love you need—and faithful friendship with sinners through the finished work of Christ on the cross. This love is the ongoing power that runs the universe and is leading you into the new heavens and new earth. The justice I bring is more than legal correctness. It involves the perfect world you've always longed for but never experienced. I am righteous in that I never fail to be perfectly God. I am all God should be and all you need for me to be, always, fully, and forever.

You are all that I need; in fact, more than I need. You have replaced my worldly enthusiasm for the things I do not really need with worthy enthusiasm for your unfailing love, your sure justice, your perfect righteousness invading this earth and my life . . .

I Am Giving You Opportunities to Grow

Dear brothers and sisters, when troubles come your way, consider it an opportunity for great joy. For you know that when your faith is tested, your endurance has a chance to grow. So let it grow, for when your endurance is fully developed, you will be perfect and complete, needing nothing.   James 1:2-4

I'm well aware of your preferred method for growing as a Christian. You would like to grow by learning more, by having a greater understanding of the Bible. And certainly you will grow as you discover me more deeply in my Word. But this is not my preferred method of helping you to grow. My chosen method for making you into a mature believer is for you to face difficulties, and for you to persevere through those difficulties with the faith I give to you. In this way your roots will go deeper and your joy will become less fleeting.

The suffering in which you persevere, fight for joy, grab hold of me, and dig deeper into my Word to understand—this is the suffering, the perseverance, that will make you spiritually mature.

Don't let me waste my suffering, Lord, by fighting against it or trying to pray it away. Give me eyes to see how you want to use it to help me grow . . .

I Will Not Forget You

Jerusalem says, "The LORD has deserted us; the Lord has forgotten us." "Never! Can a mother forget her nursing child? Can she feel no love for the child she has borne? But even if that were possible, I would not forget you! See, I have written your name on the palms of my hands. Always in my mind is a picture of Jerusalem's walls in ruins."   Isaiah 49:14-16

When hard times come, you may think you've been forgotten, that I am unaware of your heartache and uninvolved in your life. But I have bound myself to you in covenant love, and I could never forget you. I could never stop caring about your suffering or supplying your needs.

I am watching over you and thinking of you always. When I see your name written on my hand, your concerns become my concerns. I see not only your name but also every aspect of your life—every joy, every struggle, and every need. You are never off my mind, out of my sight, or away from my loving care.

When I think you are distant and do not care, I need only picture your hands, see my name written there, and remember that I am always before you because of your covenant love . . .

I Will Remove Your Idols One by One

Dear children, keep away from anything that might take God's place in your hearts.   1 John 5:21

There is nothing wrong with wanting something that is good. The problem comes when you want it too much—when a good thing becomes an ultimate thing, when a desire becomes a demand.

What is it that has become more important to you than me? What do you daydream about that brings you more plea-sure than meditating on me? What are you depending on for security and comfort instead of me? What is it that you think you cannot be happy without? Can't you see that though it may be a good thing, it has supplanted the place in your heart and life reserved for me? Can you see that it will ultimately disappoint you and even enslave you?

Won't you just name it for what it is—an idol —and let me root it out of your life? Life with me will be a process of identifying and confessing your idols one by one. I will remove them bit by bit from your heart until finally you are convinced that I am all you need to make you truly happy.

I love my idols, Lord, and it is so hard to release them. But I know that you do not withhold any good thing from me, and so I'm letting go . . .

I Will Not Let You Settle for Shallow Religiosity

You hypocrites! Isaiah was right when he prophesied about you, for he wrote, "These people honor me with their lips, but their hearts are far from me. Their worship is a farce, for they teach man-made ideas as commands from God." Matthew 15:7-9

You are to worship me. But worship, for some, can be a series of actions or words—bowing down, singings songs, saying prayers—with no engagement of the mind and emotions. I'm not interested in your going through the motions with little thought and no feeling. True worship is an affair of the heart. I'm not looking for rote applause provoked by external expectations. I long for genuine praise that comes from authentic internal appreciation.

Your highest worship begins with being broken over your sin. Mingled with genuine contrition is the feeling of longing or desire for me as well as fear of me, gratitude toward me, and joy in me. When these feelings are quickened, your worship moves beyond lip service to a heart and mind reality. What joy—for me and for you—when you worship me in this way.

I do not want to settle for the dryness of going through the motions of worship without my heart being touched and changed . . .

I Will Give You the Crown of Life

God blesses those who patiently endure testing and temptation.
Afterward they will receive the crown of life that God has
promised to those who love him.   James 1:12

While royal crowns may be covered in diamonds, pearls, sapphires, emeralds, and rubies, these crowns will not compare with the crown you will receive. I will reward your faithfulness in resisting temptation and your perseverance in the face of persecution. This crown is the gift I will present you for loving me more than the things of the world. You will find this crown precious because it will have cost you something, and yet you will gladly part with it. One day you will lay your crown before my throne, saying, "You are worthy, O Lord our God, to receive glory and honor and power."

On that day, your sacrifices won't seem so sacrificial, and your suffering won't seem so significant. You will recognize that I am the One who gave you the faith and the perseverance. I am the One who created in you everything that earned the crown. It all came from me, and it will be your crowning joy to lay it before me.

What a great day it will be to give you all the glory you deserve.
I will gladly lay my crown at your feet . . .

I Will Bless You by Reigning over You

May your Kingdom come soon.
May your will be done on earth,
    as it is in heaven.   Matthew 6:10

My blessing comes down to you in the form of my Kingdom, which I am establishing and inviting you to enter. Its royal culture will be better than any human accomplishment, and my righteous reign will be better than your slavery to self-rule. Self is a cruel taskmaster who can never be satisfied. I am the only Lord and Master who will forgive you when you fail me and dignify you when you obey me. My royal dominion over you is how I will save you from your slavery to self-righteousness and self-loathing.

Don't hang back with a wait-and-see attitude as I stand before you offering the infinite joys of my Kingdom rule. Yield yourself to me. Getting a taste of my goodness will empower you to spit out the sins of rebellion and self-determination from your mouth. My sweetness will overcome your deep resistance to my lordship.

Now I see that you are coming with a Kingdom of forgiveness, life, and joy, and I would be a fool to resist your rule over my life . . .

I Will Send a Helper to You

I will send you the Advocate—the Spirit of truth. He will come to you from the Father and will testify all about me. John 15:26

When your faith in me is challenged or questioned, do you wonder where you'll find the courage to stand clearly for Christ when it would be so much easier to be vague? Where you will find the words to express the truth about Christ when you still have questions yourself? My Spirit will give you what you need. You are not on your own. I have given you my Spirit as Helper, Comforter, Counselor, Advocate. He is bearing witness to the world that it has misjudged Jesus.

My Spirit is at work in the world today disturbing people's consciences and awakening new thoughts of Christ. All you need to do is step into the flow of my power. As you speak the truth about Christ, my Spirit provides the persuasion, the sense of truth down deep in the heart where the decisions of a lifetime are forged.

Holy Spirit, what a relief to know that you are the invisible third person in every conversation. You are the chief witness for Christ in the world today. So do your work in the world and through me, Spirit, spreading the truth about Christ . . .

I Will Take Away Your Shame

The man and his wife were both naked, but they felt no shame.
Genesis 2:25

I know that hiding comes very naturally to you. You learned it from your parents, Adam and Eve, who hid from me in the Garden when they turned away from me to try to have their desires met. But you do not need to hide from me. I am not seeking you out to punish you but to bless you. You can come out of hiding because Christ has covered you with his own goodness. He took upon himself your shame. So when you are ashamed of who you are and what you've done, don't run away and hide from me in fear. Instead, run toward me and confess it, and you'll be met with abundant mercy and tender forgiveness.

You always seem to be seeking after me, Lord, even when I've done what I know displeases you. Keep reminding me of your mercy and grace. Keep calling me out of the dark places where I hide from you . . .

I Am Helping You to Understand My Love

May you have the power to understand, as all God's people should, how wide, how long, how high, and how deep his love is. May you experience the love of Christ, though it is too great to understand fully. Ephesians 3:18-19

Some people go through this life never truly understanding what it is to be known intimately and yet loved purely and completely. But not you. I am providing you with an ever-deepening understanding of how magnificently you are loved. You are learning that my love for you is not merely a commitment to your comfort or your temporal happiness, but to your increasing holiness and your eternal joy. As you fix your gaze on the wonder of the Cross, the intensity and adequacy of my love is penetrating your very soul. In this way, you are not only understanding my love in an intellectual sense, you are experiencing it in a personal sense. And it is changing you.

Because I am so thoroughly and wonderfully loved by my Creator, Redeemer, Savior, I don't have to spin my wheels earning and keeping your attention and affection. I am letting you love me in the very best ways . . .

I Forgive and Forget

I will forgive their wickedness,
and I will never again remember their sins.
Jeremiah 31:34

I do not look at your sin and simply say that it doesn't matter, that it's no big deal. When I said I would forgive your wickedness, I knew what it would cost. I knew that the price for forgiveness would be paid through the death of my own Son. But this is *my* plan, my remedy for your problem of guilt. I have provided the necessary and sufficient sacrifice so that I can offer you abundant forgiveness. Will you receive this forgiveness from me? Will you enjoy the blessing of walking as one who has been forgiven?

Not only do I forgive you, I offer you the complete freedom of knowing that I will never again remember your sin. This doesn't mean that I actually forget what you've done. This means that I will no longer hold it against you. I recall what you've done, but I will never throw your failure back in your face. I will not treat you as your sins deserve. I will treat you as if you had not sinned against me.

You have every right to remind me of all my past failures, yet you keep whispering reminders of your love and acceptance . . .

My Spirit Has Set You Apart

God the Father knew you and chose you long ago, and his Spirit has made you holy. As a result, you have obeyed him and have been cleansed by the blood of Jesus Christ.   1 Peter 1:2

Long ago I chose to set you apart for myself. I set holiness as the goal of your life, the target you are to aim for. The generous nature of my grace does not make holy living optional. I do not set holiness out for you and then neglect to expect it. My grace doesn't provide an excuse for living apart from me, but rather it gives power for living as one who is set apart to me. The evidence that you are becoming holy is not merely your moral behavior. It's that your thoughts, your actions, and your desires are becoming more centered on me and what is pleasing to me.

When I say that I want you to be holy, it doesn't mean that I expect you to be perfect in the here and now. I am moving you in that direction and will complete the process when Christ returns. But even now, you can commit yourself to becoming closer in reality to what I have already declared you to be through your connectedness to Christ.

Only your grace at work in me can empower me to become holy, as you are holy . . .

I Am Giving You the Want-To

"This is the new covenant I will make with the people of Israel on that day," says the LORD. "I will put my instructions deep within them, and I will write them on their hearts."
Jeremiah 31:33

I delivered my old covenant on tablets of stone, and I instructed the Israelites to write my law on their foreheads, put it on their doorposts, and teach it to their children. But it was all on the outside. It was on the tablets and on their walls, but not in their hearts. They knew what I wanted, but they didn't have the will or the power to obey. They didn't have the "want-to."

But I am not looking for outward conformity; I want internal transformation. I hate rigid religious rituals enacted by people whose hearts are far from me. I want you to be alive on the inside—alive to me and my ways and my Word, alive with the joy of knowing me, alive with the desire to please me. So I have made a new covenant with you. I have put my law in your mind and on your heart. I am giving you the want-to. My Spirit dwelling within you moves you away from following a list of rules and into loving relationship.

Lord, carve your Word deep into my heart. I cannot work up the desire to please you on my own. I need this desire as a gift of your grace . . .

I Am with You Always

Be sure of this: I am with you always, even to the end of the age.
Matthew 28:20

I know this situation you're going through can cause you to wonder if I have abandoned you. But you can be confident that I will never turn away from you or leave you on your own. Anything and everything that could come between you and me was placed on Christ when he hung on the cross. It was then that I turned away from him—but only so I would never have to turn away from you. I abandoned him on that day so I can open my arms to you forever. And I will never let you go.

Even though you may sometimes feel as if you are on your own, your feelings don't tell the whole story. You are not alone. I am with you always—in every situation and in every moment. In your darkest, lowest experience, I am right beside you. When everyone else falls away, I will still be here. So you don't have to be afraid.

Whenever you feel alone, remember that I'm here with you, even now, and I will never leave you.

What a comfort it is to know that I am never truly alone.
Though I will one day be forced to let go of everything in this
life, you will never let go of me . . .

I Will Always Do What Is Right

Should not the Judge of all the earth do what is right?
Genesis 18:25

Sometimes what I do or don't do does not seem right or fair to you. You like to think that you are an expert on justice—that you have the ability to determine what is right in this world. But the more you see my true, perfect, and pure justice, the more you will realize that you don't begin to have the wisdom and perspective to exercise impeccable judgment in this world. My righteous judgment is the plumb line that all justice is judged against.

In a world of corruption, I cannot be corrupted. In a world of compromise, I will stand firm. I need no additional testimony, and I am not missing any important evidence. I will not deal with you unfairly or too harshly. I will do what is right.

As my pure justice works its way into what you understand and assume about me, rather than questioning my timing or doubting my goodness, you can stand back and say, "God, you were right. Everything you do is right."

Forgive me, Lord, for thinking I know better than you what is right and good. Of course you will do what is right. You will do right by me . . .

You Will See All My Glory

Father, I want these whom you have given me to be with me where I am. Then they can see all the glory you gave me because you loved me even before the world began! . . . I have revealed you to them, and I will continue to do so. Then your love for me will be in them, and I will be in them.   John 17:24, 26

I want you to be with me where I am. That is why I've gone to prepare a place for you and will come back for you. But my purposes do not stop with simply having you in my presence. Your greatest joy in being with me, and therefore the thing I want you to look forward to most as you think about that day, will be in seeing my divine glory and loving me with the same intensity and integrity that I have for Christ.

I know you love me now. But when that day comes, every hindrance to your affection for me will be gone. I will enlarge your capacity to love so that you will love Christ with the same love I have for him. Imagine it. Long for it. Nurture it even now.

Father, I long to love Christ like you do, and how I look forward to the day when your love for Christ is in me. This is the love I have longed for . . .

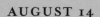

I Will Always Pursue You

I can never get away from your presence! If I go up to heaven, you are there; if I go down to the grave, you are there. If I ride the wings of the morning, if I dwell by the farthest oceans, even there your hand will guide me, and your strength will support me.   Psalm 139:7-10

As you live in a world in which so much is constantly changing, there is one constant: My presence is always with you wherever you go. My connection to you is not casual. Wherever you are, you can be certain that I am there with you.

You can never wander so far away from me that I cannot find you. You can never sin so rebelliously that I will not forgive you. You can never gain enough knowledge to surpass me. You can never gather enough resources that you won't need me.

The world around you will never drown out my voice so that you cannot hear me. The darkness will never envelop you so completely that you cannot see me.

What have I ever done to deserve such a faithful love? Your intimate knowledge of me and passionate pursuit of me is far more blessing than I could ever deserve . . .

See My Smile on You

May the LORD smile on you and be gracious to you.
Numbers 6:25

Are you sometimes afraid to really look to me, afraid that you will see a face painted with disappointment, eyes that burn with anger, or a frown of disapproval?

Oh, my child, look to me and see my smile on your life. See my radiant joy over you. My face is turned toward you in grace—and it is radiant because I see you not for who you are on your own, but for who you are in Christ. I am not focused on what you have done, good or bad, but on what Christ has done. Because you are in Christ, you need never fear to turn toward me even when you've done wrong. Look to me and see my smile toward you. My grace is waiting for you when you turn away from what brings you shame and regret and turn toward me.

Sometimes it's hard for me to believe that your face lights up when you look on me. But that's because I persist in believing it is up to me to be good enough for you rather than depending on Christ to be good enough for you. I turn now toward your radiant face . . .

I Am Enabling You to Live a Life Worthy of My Call

We keep on praying for you, asking our God to enable you to live a life worthy of his call. May he give you the power to accomplish all the good things your faith prompts you to do.
2 Thessalonians 1:11

You know what my Spirit has been prompting you to do, yet so far you have not moved. Don't you know that I will give you the power to do anything I've put before you to do?

This is how you live day to day in a manner that is worthy of one I call my own—through the active engagement of your will, you resolve to do what pleases me, forsake what you know is displeasing, and depend on my power. I'm not interested in mere morality accomplished apart from me. It is my glory that is at stake, and my power that will make this kind of living possible. Examine yourself today for what is unfitting, unworthy of your calling. As you engage your will, you will find that I will provide the power to rid your life of these things and replace them with invigorating joy and relief.

Show me what is improper, unfit, and inappropriate for a life in which you dwell. Bless me today with power so I can live a life worthy of your call . . .

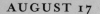
I Have Satisfied My Conscience Concerning You

Let us go right into the presence of God with sincere hearts fully trusting him. For our guilty consciences have been sprinkled with Christ's blood to make us clean, and our bodies have been washed with pure water. Hebrews 10:22

What is weighing down your conscience today? If it is unconfessed sin, simply lay it out before me and I will wipe it away. I will heal you from the damage it has done. My Spirit will go to work, diminishing your desire to sin in this way again.

But if it is sin you have confessed that is weighing you down, why are you still carrying it around? Don't you know that at the Cross I satisfied my own conscience in regard to your sin? And, knowing that, can't your conscience be satisfied too? Certainly my standards are higher than yours, and I have met my standards for you through Christ. So you can put your past away, because I have put it away.

Don't let your conscience continue to accuse you. Be forgiven. Be released. Come alive. Live again.

I will not linger here far away from you, stewing in my shame. You are giving me a heart that is confident in your mercy. So I am drawing near, expecting to be accepted, not condemned . . .

I Bless Those Who Tremble at My Word

I will bless those who have humble and contrite hearts, who
tremble at my word.   Isaiah 66:2

Many people in the world hear my Word and simply ignore
it. Some reduce it into something manageable, and others
set themselves above it. But not you. This is how you know
and I know you are mine, living in the overflow of my blessing: Your soul hungers for my Word and can be satisfied with
nothing less.

You have set no preconditions and erected no boundaries
in your life, but have opened it up wholly and humbly to be
purified by my holy Word. You have turned away from the
worldly voices that shout out to keep you from hearing me,
and you have tuned in to my voice with a trembling eager-
ness. Your longing to hear, your desire to believe, and your
intention to obey sets you apart and prepares you to receive
from me.

I will not come to your Word casually but with humility, in full
recognition of my neediness, my sinfulness, and my inadequacy
before you, and in full confidence of your goodness and grace. So
speak to me, Lord. Let me hear your voice . . .

I Have Saved You Because of My Mercy

When God our Savior revealed his kindness and love, he saved us, not because of the righteous things we had done, but because of his mercy. Titus 3:4-5

So many people try so hard to be good, thinking that if they can be good enough, I will accept them and bless them. But I do not bless good people for the good things they do; I bless bad people in spite of the bad things they have done. I delight in showing mercy to people who turn to me because they realize that apart from Christ, they simply can't be good enough to be worthy of my blessing. My blessing is not that I accept their efforts at being good, but that I credit them with Christ's own goodness.

Aren't you glad that your salvation does not depend on your own goodness but on my mercy? Instead of scrambling to do more, rest in the work of Christ who has done everything. Instead of pointing to your record of good deeds, look at the revelation of my kindness and love.

Nothing could make me humbler or happier than the truth that I have been born again, not because of anything I did, but because of your mercy . . .

I Have Made My Word Understandable to You

The teaching of your word gives light, so even the simple can understand.   Psalm 119:130

My Word is a treasure of knowledge to be mined and explored. It provides level after deeper level of understanding. But this does not mean that you need an advanced degree or special experience to understand it. Everything you need for salvation and for living as mine is clear in the Scripture.

Understanding the Bible is more of a spiritual endeavor than an intellectual ability, having more to do with your heart than your mental capacity. As you come to my Word in earnest to learn of me and abide in me, you can trust me to open your mind so you can grasp what you read. So when you come to something in my Word that you don't understand, see that I am giving you a fresh opportunity to discover something about me. Ask for my help and search my Word intently, believing that I will show you what you need to learn.

You have condescended to reveal yourself in human language, making the grand mystery of who you are and what you are doing in this world understandable to even me . . .

I Am with You to Comfort and Correct You

Even when I walk through the darkest valley, I will not be afraid, for you are close beside me. Your rod and your staff protect and comfort me.   Psalm 23:4

I take care of my children in adversity. When the darkness is closing in, look up and see that I am leading you, and refuse to give in to fear.

When I see you heading in the wrong direction, toward things that appear to be fulfilling and harmless but are really depleting and destructive, I love you too much to let you keep going. So I reach out to draw you back to the safety of my presence as my Spirit speaks conviction. You may think I've frustrated your perfectly good plans or that I'm curtailing your innocent fun. But remember that I'm out in front of you throughout this life, guiding you along paths that will lead you where I know you truly want to go. And I'm also behind you, pursuing you with my goodness and unfailing love so that you will make your home in me now and forevermore.

My Shepherd, my Lord, keep using your rod of discipline and your staff that draws me away from danger. Keep leading and pursuing me all the days of my life . . .

My Greatest Command Brings Your Greatest Joy

Jesus answered, "The most important is, 'Hear, O Israel: The Lord our God, the Lord is one. And you shall love the Lord your God with all your heart and with all your soul and with all your mind and with all your strength.'" Mark 12:29-30, ESV

My commands are not burdensome. They do not diminish your happiness but make it more solid, less fleeting. In fact, as you obey my greatest command, you will find your greatest joy.

Love me. Love me from the heart, not as an obligation or duty, but by treasuring and adoring me. Love me from your soul, allowing me to fill its aching corners. Love me with your mind by refusing to settle for a vague understanding of who I am and what I'm about in the world.

Loving me is an affair of the passions of your heart, the longings of your soul, the ponderings of your mind. As you focus on the Cross, loving me will lose any sense of duty as my clearest demonstration of love for you melts your heart, stirs your soul, and changes your perspective.

In light of your greatest command, I see my greatest sin—not loving you as you deserve and desire. And so I look to the Cross, and my heart is melted once again . . .

I Am Coming to Call You

The Lord himself will come down from heaven with a commanding shout. . . . First, the Christians who have died will rise from their graves. Then, together with them, we who are still alive and remain on the earth will be caught up in the clouds to meet the Lord in the air. Then we will be with the Lord forever. 1 Thessalonians 4:16-17

Though your body may one day be put into a grave, your final destiny is not the grave but glory. I do not intend for you to spend eternity in a faraway place populated by disembodied spirits. To be absent from your body and at home with me will be wonderful, but it is not your ultimate hope.

Your hope is this—that your body will be raised so that you will have the joy of physically meeting Christ in the air upon his return and welcoming him to his kingdom. You will be with the risen Christ with a body like his own glorious body. Your final destiny and eternal state is to reign with Christ on the renewed earth.

This is the truth with which we are to encourage each other, and so I am swallowing it whole, asking you to make it real to me. Make this resurrection reality the foundation of my hope . . .

I Want You to Be Continually Connected to Me

I am the vine; you are the branches. Those who remain in me, and I in them, will produce much fruit. For apart from me you can do nothing. John 15:5

While your default setting may be to live for me, I'm inviting you to live in me. Your connection to me allows the life of Jesus to flow fruitfully through you. This is not one brand of Christianity for the super spiritual, but the essence of all genuine relationship to me.

As you remain in me, I will turn even the moments of fear and frustration in your life into a miracle. When personalities around you are grating on you, remain in me. When the doctor calls with unwelcome test results, remain in me. When everyone is congratulating you for a job well done, remain in me. As you struggle against your stubborn will, remain in me.

The cure for all of your miseries is not within you. As you remain in me, I am making you into my miracle.

The day will come, Lord, when all of the other concerns of this life will no longer matter. But one thing will grow in grandeur as I sail off into eternity—my life-giving connectedness to you . . .

My Grace Is Taking Away Your Taste for Sin

Since God's grace has set us free from the law, does that mean we can go on sinning? Of course not! Romans 6:15

My gift of grace is not a free pass for sinful indulgence, but a transforming power for saying no to sin. My grace is abundant and free, but that does not mean that you can sin as much as you want. My grace at work in your life means that you don't have to sin and, increasingly, you don't want to.

My grace has saved you not only from the punishment and guilt that come from sin but also from its presence and practice, its destruction, its false promises, its heartbreak, and its painful consequences.

If you truly grasp the generosity of my grace, you recognize that I have opened myself up to be taken advantage of. But because your faith is real, taking advantage of my grace is, to you, inconceivable. Its power has gone to work in you, changing you. You are losing your taste and appetite for sin.

Your grace has put a claim upon me, and it is energizing me to live all out for you and love it . . .

When You Call, I Will Answer

Free those who are wrongly imprisoned; lighten the burden of those who work for you. . . . Share your food with the hungry, and give shelter to the homeless. Give clothes to those who need them. . . . Then when you call, the LORD will answer. "Yes, I am here," he will quickly reply. Isaiah 58:6-7, 9

I love you too much to let you settle for some sense of false religiosity. So I am calling you to authentic spirituality. Here is how you live out real faith before me: you get your eyes off yourself, your concerns, your struggles, your needs, and you throw yourself into meeting the needs of others.

As you become the answer to someone else's prayers, you will look up and discover that I am answering your prayers. As you give yourself away, you will discover that you have been blessed with more than you could ever ask for. We'll have the real relationship you long for, and when you call to me, you will find me humbly available and quickly responsive.

Lord, I don't want to waste my life caught up in my own concerns. I want to give my life away as your representative in this hurting world . . .

I Will Not Let Your Faith Fail

Simon, Simon, Satan has asked to sift each of you like wheat. But I have pleaded in prayer for you, Simon, that your faith should not fail. So when you have repented and turned to me again, strengthen your brothers. Luke 22:31-32

You have an enemy who wants to sift you like wheat. He wants to put you through the wringer to destroy your faith and confidence in me. He wants to make you think that you have strayed beyond the bounds of my love and forgiveness, so you'll be too ashamed to return to me.

But you are not at the mercy of your great enemy. Your great Mediator, Jesus Christ, has pleaded in prayer for you, that though you may stumble, you will not fall. And because he has prayed for you, though you may falter in this life of faith, you will not ultimately fail.

Satan may send suffering in an effort to destroy your faith, but you need to know that I intend to use it to develop your faith. What he sends to tempt, I use to train. What he sends to wound you, I will use to prune you.

I have failed again, but I'm turning back to you, knowing that you are the One who keeps me from falling away . . .

I Have Goodness Stored Up for You

How great is the goodness you have stored up for those who
fear you. You lavish it on those who come to you for protection,
blessing them before the watching world.   Psalm 31:19

I am a God to be feared, and I bless those who fear me. The
fear I require should not cause you to run away from me but
compel you to run toward me. This fear makes you want to
run to me for power to forsake sin, and mercy, which provides
pardon for sin.

Because you fear me, you don't have to run from me in
terror of my rejection or wrath, and neither do you need to
run away to satisfy your longings or relieve your anxieties.
Instead, as you wait for me, hope in me, and stay close to me,
the prospect of running down a path of sin is too frightening
to pursue, and the benefits of abiding in the shadow of my
almightiness are too glorious to forsake.

Because I fear you, Lord, I'm not running away from you but
toward you. All the protection I have needed from you because
of my sin has been provided by you in Christ. So instead of
storing up punishment for me, you have stored up goodness
and you lavish it on me . . .

I Am Giving You the Faith You Need

Faith is the confidence that what we hope for will actually happen; it gives us assurance about things we cannot see.
Hebrews 11:1

I am giving you the faith you need to become convinced that everything I have told you and promised you is really true. This faith invites you to step out to follow a God you have never seen with your eyes or heard with your ears, trusting in a reality that the collective voice of the world says does not exist and does not matter.

Faith is believing that there is something more durable, more dependable, and more delightful than anything in this world. Faith is believing that something more can be found only in me—and then living like you believe it.

You can be confident that what you hope for, based on what you have read in my Word, will actually happen. Though it is not yet realized, it is certain. You haven't experienced it all yet, but there is no question that you will. There is no real risk involved in placing your hopes in my promises. You can be sure of what you hope for and certain of what you do not see.

Though I can't see it yet with my physical eyes, one day I will see it all, enjoy it all, and thank you once again for the faith to believe . . .

I Will Turn Your Losses into Gains

If you try to hang on to your life, you will lose it. But if you give up your life for my sake, you will save it. Matthew 16:25

Your enemy has planted the idea in your head that I cannot be trusted—that if you give yourself to me you will lose out on all there is to enjoy in life. But don't believe it. I do not want to take away all that you hold dear; I simply want to become your most prized possession. I want you to see that I am more precious and more satisfying than anything or anyone else, and I want to give myself to you.

The apostle Paul discovered that everything he once thought was valuable was in fact worthless when compared with the priceless gain of knowing Christ. He moved what he had seen as assets into the liability column of his life, and he reordered his entire life in order to get what he valued most.

As you grow in recognition of how much Christ is worth, your superstitions will dissolve into sweet surrender. You'll be glad to let go of anything that keeps you from enjoying more of me.

I see that losing what I love in this life does not mean losing out. You are turning my temporary losses into eternal gains . . .

I Am Refining You

I have refined you, but not as silver is refined. Rather, I have refined you in the furnace of suffering. Isaiah 48:10

You are being afflicted now, but not forever. However long your trials may seem to last, they will surely come to an end—a profitable end.

I employ the furnace of affliction not to ruin but to refine the faith of my people. I want to burn away your doubts and distractions, your stubborn rebellions and harmful addictions, your perverted ambitions and petty animosities. As all of these impurities burn away, the image of my Son will be more clearly revealed in you.

Though you may find yourself on the anvil of suffering, I have not abandoned you and I am not being cruel to you. I am at work. I know just how hot the fire should be and how long you must be in it. I am extracting all of the impurities from you to fit you for an eternity in my presence in heaven.

Patient Refiner, plunge me into the fires of difficulty if you must. I am trusting that the fires will not leave me deformed but transformed into the image of your Son . . .

I Will Judge You according to the Book

I saw the dead, both great and small, standing before God's throne. And the books were opened, including the Book of Life. And the dead were judged according to what they had done, as recorded in the books. Revelation 20:12

The day will come when I will open the books, which hold a record of the deeds of all people. For those who have not trusted in Christ but are hoping that their good deeds will outweigh their bad deeds and get them into heaven, the books will bring condemnation. But for you, the books will provide confirmation that you are connected to Christ in a saving, transforming way.

The books will show how you threw yourself on my mercy, how you welcomed my forgiveness, and how your appetites and affections changed as my Spirit went to work in you. The books will provide an accounting of all the things God's grace in your life has empowered you to do and become because of your connectedness to Jesus. You will not be judged according to the books but on the basis of the Book of Life, where your name has been written by my own hand.

My deeds are not the basis of my salvation but the evidence of it. I do not have to fear not measuring up. Christ is my righteousness . . .

I Am Giving You Reason to Trust My Promises

God also bound himself with an oath, so that those who received the promise could be perfectly sure that he would never change his mind.   Hebrews 6:17

I see that you've gone out on a limb. You're staking your reputation, your life, your future on the promises I have made to you. I assure you that you will never regret it. The day will never come when you think yourself a fool for putting all of your hopes in what I have promised you.

My Word is sure and certain. But I know you live in a world where people make promises all the time that they do not keep. So while I didn't have to swear by an oath, I did, to accommodate your doubts. I have bound myself with an oath to provide you with every confidence so that you can grab hold of my promises in a world of broken promises. I have sworn on the highest, most honorable name I can swear on— my own. My oath is meant to give you deep confidence that I will not change my mind about you. You will inherit all I have promised to you through Christ.

Through faith, I'm taking hold of your promises as my own. Though I am unable to keep all of the promises I have made to you, you will keep your promises to me, and that is enough . . .

I Infuse Your Life with Meaning

My dear brothers and sisters, be strong and immovable. Always work enthusiastically for the Lord, for you know that nothing you do for the Lord is ever useless. 1 Corinthians 15:58

An abundant life is a life that has meaning and purpose. And I know that is what you want. You don't want to simply watch the days and years go by, collecting a few more things, going a few more places, and saving a few more dollars, with no sense that it matters for eternity.

As you unashamedly talk about me, your words are made fruitful. As you earn and invest money in Kingdom endeavors, you store up treasure that will last forever. I see you serve in ways that no one ever esteems or notices. I see the extra care you invest in your efforts because you work as if you are working directly for me. I see the integrity you show when no one would know otherwise. And so I am blessing your life with a satisfying sense of purpose. I am infusing all your efforts with meaning.

When I think I am wasting my time and effort, I look to you, Lord, confident that you will not let my labor for you go to waste . . .

I Give You the Pleasure of Joining Me in My Work

He is the God who made the world and everything in it. Since he is Lord of heaven and earth, he doesn't live in man-made temples, and human hands can't serve his needs—for he has no needs. He himself gives life and breath to everything, and he satisfies every need. Acts 17:24-25

Don't believe it for a minute when someone tells you that I created mankind because I was lonely, or that my plans for the world can be frustrated by those who don't cooperate.

I have no needs, nor do I depend on any lesser creature for anything. I do not need helpers. However, I do stoop to work in and through my beloved and obedient children for their joy. I am giving you the pleasure of joining me in my work in this world. I have chosen to use you for my purposes and for your joy.

I was not lonely. After all, the Father, Son, and Spirit have always enjoyed perfect and complete fellowship. I made you in my image to enjoy me and glorify me. I determined that you would be meaningful to me, which is the very definition of significance.

You, Lord, are all-sufficient in yourself; there is no deficiency in you. I praise you and thank you for inviting me into your work and into your fellowship . . .

I Have Shown You My Favor

May the LORD show you his favor and give you his peace.
Numbers 6:26

I want you to hear me speaking over you the same words I spoke over my Son: "This is my dearly loved Son, who brings me great joy." You are my dearly loved child, and you bring me great joy.

Is it hard for you to imagine? Does it seem undeserved? That is exactly what grace is—undeserved favor. This is the favor I am showing to you today. Because you have hidden yourself in Christ, the Son who brings me great joy, you bring me great joy.

No longer do you live under my frown. Instead, you are showered by my favor. No longer are you alienated from me because of your sin. My Son has made peace with me on your behalf. So enjoy my favor today. Rest in my peace. Live as one who is dearly loved by your heavenly Father—because you are.

Jesus, you absorbed God's anger toward sin so that I can enjoy his unending favor. What goodness, what grace, so undeserved . . .

I Have Broken the Power of Sin in Your Life

Since we have been united with him in his death, we will also be raised to life as he was. We know that our old sinful selves were crucified with Christ so that sin might lose its power in our lives. We are no longer slaves to sin. Romans 6:5-6

Sin once had supreme power in your life. Its power was in its promises of pleasure. But its promises always prove false, and its pleasures are always fleeting. In the end, sin only depletes and destroys. And this is why I want you to be done with sin, to live in freedom as one who has been saved from the clutches of this evil taskmaster.

Use your freedom to run in the opposite direction of sin. Run toward me, listening to my voice, seeking after my ways, enjoying my presence. Begin to live out the reality of this new life you have, united to Christ, by saying no when sin tries to pull you back into old ways of thinking, relating, and acting. Sin wants only to rob you of freedom and joy, not provide it to you.

How can I keep living like a slave when you have paid my ransom and given me a whole new life? You have set me free, Lord, and I want to run in your direction . . .

I Have Given You a Worthwhile Goal

Whether we are here in this body or away from this body, our goal is to please him.   2 Corinthians 5:9

So much happens in your life that you cannot control. But I have given you a place to put your focus and invest your energies in the midst of a world you cannot control. Your life is not merely about securing the hope of heaven and then living as you please. As you wait for heaven, throw everything you have and everything you are into this singular aim: Make it your goal to please me. Set your sights on living a life that honors me and on becoming a person who is pleasing to me.

When hard things come (and they will) and you wonder what to do, make it your goal to please me in how you respond. When you are betrayed, abandoned, or misused, invest your energies in pleasing me instead of justifying yourself. When you feel the sting of undeserved criticism, the fearfulness of being alone, the weight of overwhelming responsibility, or the aimlessness that comes from lack of purpose or significance, make it your goal to please me.

Oh, Lord, how I long to please you in how I invest my time and money, how I handle success as well as failure. Thank you for filling my life with meaning by giving me this worthwhile goal . . .

You Will Be Recognized as Mine

God blesses those who work for peace, for they will be called the children of God. Matthew 5:9

I am a peace-loving God and a peacemaking God. My heaven is a place of peace. So when you operate in the world, in your church, in your home as a peacemaker, it becomes obvious that I am your Father. I have made peace with sinners through the Cross, and my children are recognizable by their willingness to make sacrifices for peace as I have.

As a peacemaker, you will love your enemies instead of constantly throwing more logs on the fire of your anger toward them. You'll pray blessings on those who persecute you instead of mumbling curses under your breath. You'll choose again and again to let my love toward you overflow into your relationships so that you will not always be nursing an injury, obsessing over a slight, or taking offense so easily. You'll build bridges to people rather than settle into a comfortable distance. You will persevere in becoming reconciled whenever there has been a rupture in relationship.

I could have no greater joy than to be told that I look like you, my Father, in the way I make peace with those around me . . .

I Am Slow to Anger with You

The LORD passed in front of Moses, calling out, "Yahweh! The LORD! The God of compassion and mercy! I am slow to anger and filled with unfailing love and faithfulness."   Exodus 34:6

All that I am as God I am to you. I am compassionate. I care about your situation, and I am sympathetic with your weakness. My heart is drawn to help you whenever you are in need. I am the God of mercy. Rather than giving you what you deserve because of your sin—condemnation—I am giving you what you don't deserve—salvation. I am slow to anger, not capricious or volatile. When I act against evil, I do it righteously and deliberately, not out of an uncontrolled temper. I am not rash to act against those I have created, even when they are in rebellion against me. I wait patiently, giving sinners the opportunity to return to me in repentance.

Because my heart is not filled with frustration or anger but with unfailing love and faithfulness, you need not cower before me but can come to me. I will always follow through on my love.

You have set your love on me, and I know that it will remain constant and unchanging. You have been patient with me, and I am awash in your mercy . . .

I Will Reward You

Look, I am coming soon, bringing my reward with me to repay all people according to their deeds. Revelation 22:12

While salvation is about my work for you and is a free gift of grace to which you contribute nothing, my rewards are dependent on your faithfulness to me. Belief determines your eternal destination, but behavior determines your eternal reward.

But it is not that I saved you by my grace and then put you to work to keep earning my favor so you can stay saved. You are connected to Christ, and because of that life-giving connection, good works will naturally flow out of your life. I began a good work in you, and I will be faithful to complete it. Every bit of obedience I graciously decide to reward is a gift from me in the first place.

While everyone in heaven will be perfectly happy and completely satisfied, not every believer's position and experience will be the same. As you walk with me and live for me, I expand your capacity for eternal joy.

I live to hear you say to me, "Well done, good and faithful servant! You have been faithful with a few things; I will put you in charge of many things. Come and share your master's happiness!" . . .

SEPTEMBER 11

I Will Help You Escape the World's Corruption

Because of his glory and excellence, he has given us great and precious promises. These are the promises that enable you to share his divine nature and escape the world's corruption caused by human desires. 2 Peter 1:4

I know you are living in a world that promises you pleasure everywhere you turn. But you've tasted enough of sin's promises to know that they always turn sour in your mouth. You've listened to enough of sin's lies to know that they do not deliver. Sin makes its attack by holding out false promises of happiness to you. It tells you that if you lie on your income tax return, you'll have more money to enjoy; it says that if you get a divorce, you'll both be happier; if you brag about your accomplishment, you'll be admired; if you keep quiet about your faith, you'll get ahead.

So you must do battle at the level of your desires by hanging my promises of deep and lasting happiness like a carrot in front of your eyes. They will lure you away from sin.

As I keep before my eyes the astonishing promises you have made to me for now as well as for the life to come, your divine voice defeats sin's lies. Your divine power bends and reshapes my desires toward pleasing you . . .

I Have Secured Your Future

I saw a scroll in the right hand of the one who was sitting on the throne. There was writing on the inside and the outside of the scroll, and it was sealed with seven seals. Revelation 5:1

The scroll represents my decrees concerning what will happen in the future. You see, the future of this world is not determined by fate or chance. All of history is the unfolding of my predetermined plan for all things. What is written on the scroll is precise, and it is sealed so you will know that it is complete and cannot be altered—that it has not yet been revealed and has not yet come to pass.

When you picture me on the throne of this universe holding that sealed scroll, you can trust that my plans—not only for this world but also for your life—are precise, complete, and perfect. You can rest in knowing that a sovereign God is seated on the throne, that nothing happens in your life that is outside of my plans, and that my plans for you are good even when they don't seem that way on the surface.

The sealed scroll reminds me that you are worthy of my radical trust when the future seems uncertain. You are in absolute control and have loving plans for my future firmly in your grasp . . .

I Will Show an Unimaginable Measure of Mercy

He will pour out his anger and wrath on those who live for themselves, who refuse to obey the truth and instead live lives of wickedness.　　Romans 2:8

I do not manipulate with idle threats. I have promised to pour out my wrath, and I will not go soft. I am too perfect for that; in fact, I am perfectly just. There is a time for mercy and grace, and then at some point, when warnings have been unheeded and there is no repentance, there comes a time to follow through with the appropriate punishment. That is justice. Justice demands that evil be punished, and you can be certain that it will be. My wrath is not the irrational rage of an egotistical, power-grabbing deity but the righteous, pure, and perfectly appropriate expression of justice.

Until now, I have chosen to show mercy—an unimaginable measure of mercy. But the time for mercy will pass, and there will be no more mercy for rebellion, rejection, or refusal, and no more time for repentance. So rest in knowing that you are a recipient of my mercy and live as one who is greatly loved.

Because I belong to you, Lord, I do not have to fear being a target of your anger. I can rest in knowing that while unrepentant evil will not go unpunished, I will not be punished. Instead of wrath, you are pouring out your grace on me . . .

I Will Provide the Contentment You Crave

Don't love money; be satisfied with what you have. For God has said, "I will never fail you. I will never abandon you."
Hebrews 13:5

Even though I have given you so much, you want more. But the life of your dreams cannot be purchased with money, and it is not found in the constant pursuit of one more thing. That is a life of tyranny and dissatisfaction. The life of your dreams is found in learning to be content.

You think you'll be content when you finally get what you want. But real contentment is found when you accept something less than what you want or something other than what you want. That is real freedom. And it doesn't just happen. It must be cultivated as you tell yourself the truth about this world and about me. The truth is that the things of this world will never fully satisfy you.

Everything you can buy with money will one day fail you. But I will never fail you. Everything you collect, you will one day be forced to relinquish. But I will never let go of you.

The world tells me that I deserve better, that I've earned more. But I hear your call to a life of being content with what I have, a life of confidence in you rather than in money and what it will buy . . .

No One Can Take You from Me

My sheep listen to my voice; I know them, and they follow me.
I give them eternal life, and they will never perish. No one can
snatch them away from me. John 10:27-28

You're safe. You're secure. You are mine. How can you be sure
you are mine? Because you listen to my voice. You open up my
Word and take it in rather than explain it away; you meditate
on it and make it part of you. I know you are mine because
you follow after me rather than running from me and my
commands.

Because you are mine, you have so much life to look forward to—in quality and quantity. You are not missing out on
anything good as you follow me but are storing up goodness
for yourself. Though your body may one day die, you will
never perish. Your life will not end in the grave but will endure
in glory. Even when you give in to doubt or disobedience, do
not fear. Because you are mine, I will always woo you back to
listening to my voice and following in my footsteps.

I hear your voice and I am following you, so grateful to know
that nothing can come between us . . .

This Kind of Sorrow Will Make You Happy Forever

The kind of sorrow God wants us to experience leads us away from sin and results in salvation. There's no regret for that kind of sorrow. But worldly sorrow, which lacks repentance, results in spiritual death.   2 Corinthians 7:10

I take no pleasure when you hurt. But there is a kind of sorrow I do want you to experience—not because it will make you miserable, but because it will lead to eternal happiness. I love you so much that I am willing for you to be sad in this way.

I want you to truly mourn over your sin. You must see its filthy defilement, its bold betrayal, its destructive evil. Weep over the distance it has brought between us. Groan over the damage it has done. Let it break your heart in the best ways. This is a redemptive sadness, and you will never regret giving yourself over to it. It will become the grounds for changing direction, the impetus for genuine repentance. This sorrow will lead you to eternal joy.

Often I resist the discomfort of deep sorrow over my sin, rushing quickly past it to enjoy your generous forgiveness. But today I will linger to see my sin the way you do . . .

Coming Clean with Me Brings Healing

If we confess our sins to him, he is faithful and just to forgive us our sins and to cleanse us from all wickedness. 1 John 1:9

I know it is never comfortable when my Spirit shows you the areas of your life that are offensive to me. I'm not trying to hurt you by calling attention to your sin; I'm helping you. Won't you let me love you in this way? Just turn toward me and begin to confess those sins rather than ignoring them or trying to hide them. I won't turn away from you. I will cleanse you.

This repentance I'm calling you to is not a onetime thing. I'm asking you to make it your way of life. As you live in brokenness before me, I will continue to show you the things in your life that keep you from closer fellowship with me—not to condemn you or discourage you, but to draw you into the full and free life I have for you.

On the cross, Christ dealt decisively with your deepest and most destructive disease, and even now you are being healed by his wounds.

As I lay my broken life before you and invite you into it, you are moving toward me, doing a work of great healing and bringing me peace . . .

I Am Drawn to Your Tender Heart

Is there any encouragement from belonging to Christ? Any comfort from his love? Any fellowship together in the Spirit? Are your hearts tender and compassionate? Philippians 2:1

Some people develop a tough exterior as they go through life in this world, seeking to be invulnerable to pain. But as I work in you, my goal is not to give you thick skin so that nothing can hurt you. I do not want you to become cold, callous, and hard-hearted toward me, and neither do I want you to be insensitive to the hurts of others. To protect your heart from being broken by the things that break my heart is to have little genuine connection to me.

I am drawn to a heart that is sensitive to being touched— even though it might cause some pain. I intend for you to stay soft and tender, moldable, and even vulnerable, because this is what you need to stay responsive to me. Sensitivity to sin and tender compassion toward the hurts of others flow only out of a heart that can be broken.

Sometimes I want to build a wall around my heart and put blinders on my eyes so the pain of this world can't touch me. But your Spirit is at work in me, making my heart tender . . .

I Will Reward Your Sincere, Secret Prayer

When you pray, don't be like the hypocrites who love to pray publicly on street corners and in the synagogues where everyone can see them. I tell you the truth, that is all the reward they will ever get. But when you pray, go away by yourself, shut the door behind you, and pray to your Father in private. Then your Father, who sees everything, will reward you. Matthew 6:5-6

The world is looking for magic formulas to get good things from me. Plenty of people use public prayer to put on a spiritual show. They would much rather gain a reputation as a pray-er than do the hard work of prayer.

But you know that the real secret to prayer is secret prayer. Communing with me in prayer and finding your rest in me is itself the prize. Sincere, secret prayer is always rewarded with a response from me. While it may not always be the response you want, you can be certain that it is the best response. So come to me in private. Pour out your concerns, leaving behind all pretenses. Then you'll find your best reward, not in making an impression on others, but in finding true intimacy with me.

There could be no greater joy in this world or the next than communing in the secret place with you, the living God . . .

I Am Putting My Strength on Display in Your Life

I am glad to boast about my weaknesses, so that the power of Christ can work through me. That's why I take pleasure in my weaknesses, and in the insults, hardships, persecutions, and troubles that I suffer for Christ. For when I am weak, then I am strong. 2 Corinthians 12:9-10

I am making your life a beautiful display case for my glory. And while I know you would rather have me display my glory through your successes and strengths, that is not how I do things.

When you are obviously inadequate for the task and my power at work through you gets the job done, my strength is put on display. When your body fails you and yet you can smile, confident in my goodness, it is obvious that the power of Christ is working through you. When you endure unjust criticism without becoming defensive and when you are misunderstood without becoming bitter, the world around you cannot miss that it is my Spirit inside you that makes you strong.

Lord, I don't want to boast about my strengths but about the weak places in my life where you shine strong . . .

My Word Is Doing Its Work in Your Life

All Scripture is inspired by God and is useful to teach us what is true and to make us realize what is wrong in our lives. It corrects us when we are wrong and teaches us to do what is right. 2 Timothy 3:16

Some people search through my Word for something that appeals, something that comforts, something that inspires. But I have given it to you for so much more. You are blessed when you truly take it in—all of it—because you want to hear everything I have to say to you.

Rather than dabble in my Word, picking and choosing what interests you, you are letting my Word more than dabble in your life. You have placed yourself under it as a student and allowed my Word to teach you what is true. You've opened yourself up to it as a patient and allowed my Word to show you where your soul is sick. You have subjected yourself to it as a child and let it correct your misbehaviors and misbeliefs.

O God, go to work with your Word in my life. I'm embarrassed by my errors, so teach me what is true. I'm ashamed of what dishonors you, so teach me to do what is right . . .

I Will Make You Forever Fruitful

They delight in the law of the LORD,
*   meditating on it day and night.*
They are like trees planted along the riverbank,
*   bearing fruit each season.*
Their leaves never wither,
*   and they prosper in all they do.*   Psalm 1:2-3

As you find life in my Word and make it your way of life, your roots are going deeper and deeper in me. Deep roots are what you need when strong winds of difficulty and disappointment begin to blow in your life. You see, abundant life doesn't mean I will spare you from the hard things. It means I will be your security in the storm.

I'm not saying that you will be unaffected by the hurts this life throws your way. I'm saying that you will not be completely crushed or destroyed by them. In fact, my Spirit working in you will enable you to do far more than simply endure difficulty. I will work in you to make you fruitful right there in the middle of hard times. Out of your life will flow peace and joy and contentment because your roots go deep in me.

This blessedness sometimes seems too good to believe in, Lord,
yet I know that I can endure more today than I did when I first
found my place in you. My roots are going deeper as I go deeper
in your Word . . .

I Have Given You a Better Obsession

Let us run with endurance the race God has set before us. We do this by keeping our eyes on Jesus, the champion who initiates and perfects our faith. Hebrews 12:1-2

I have given you so many good things—so many things worthy of being enjoyed and desired. What you want is not necessarily bad. It's that you want it too much. Your desire so easily becomes a demand, and you find yourself off track, obsessed with so many lesser things than Jesus himself.

So will you let me bless you by giving you a better obsession than whatever it is that dominates your thoughts and desires? Will you make Jesus the center of your life, the focus of your thoughts, the object of your passion, the definition of your identity, the source of your significance, the supplier of your happiness? You do not want to settle for being merely affiliated with Jesus, interested in him, or associated with him. He must take center stage in your thoughts and emotions. Real blessing is found as you are united with him and as you give yourself to him, letting go of whatever keeps you from him.

I am taking stock of my ambitions, my allegiances, and my affections. I want you to be at the center, Jesus, in your rightful place . . .

I Have Provided the Weapons You Need to Win

We are human, but we don't wage war as humans do. We use God's mighty weapons, not worldly weapons, to knock down the strongholds of human reasoning and to destroy false arguments.
2 Corinthians 10:3-4

While I have assured your ultimate victory in the war for your soul, this triumph will not be accomplished without many battles and occasional defeats, wounds, and scars. So when you find yourself assaulted by a flurry of doubts, attacked by subtle temptations, or belittled by those who hate the truth, you should not be surprised. You are in a war—a war against evil rulers and authorities of the unseen world, against mighty powers in this dark world, and against evil spirits in the heavenly places. And the weapons I have provided for you to fight this war are spiritual, not natural.

I've given you prayer to fight self-sufficiency. I've given you joy to fight discouragement. I've given you truth to do battle with deceit. I've given you my Holy Spirit living inside you to overcome worldly seduction. I've given you full acceptance to silence the accusations of guilt. I've given you humble submission to defeat rebellious unbelief.

Satan seems to use every possible means to urge me to satisfy myself with anything other than Christ. But I am not at his mercy . . .

I Will Not Pour Out My Anger on You

God chose to save us through our Lord Jesus Christ, not to pour out his anger on us.   1 Thessalonians 5:9

I am not a God who has gone soft on sin. I cannot overlook it or sweep it under the rug of the universe. And you don't want me to. You want a God who is just, a God you can be certain will punish evil in this world.

But you are also well aware of the evil inside of you. While you know that you deserve to be punished for your sin, you need not live in that fear. I am not going to give you what you deserve. I gave Christ what you deserve at the Cross.

I have chosen to save you through Christ. While I poured out my anger on him, I have poured out my mercy on you. I am abundant in mercy beyond what you can conceive, and because you are in Christ, you will know only my loving embrace, not my anger.

God, this salvation from what I deserve and your decision to give me what I don't deserve is too good for me to conceive or explain, but I receive it by faith and celebrate . . .

I Am Calling You Away from Your Busyness

After sending [the people] home, [Jesus] went up into the hills by himself to pray.   Matthew 14:23

I know you are busy. I am well aware of all of the demands and interests that clamor for your attention. As soon as you finish one project, the next one is looming. Much of what you do is good. But I am calling you away from many good things to enjoy the best thing: time with me—time listening to me by reading and meditating on my Word, time talking to me about the things that really matter to you, time to simply enjoy the peace and joy of my presence.

When you read your e-mail or your newspaper before you read my Word, can you see that you are allowing them to take precedence over me? The tyranny of constant communication with the world can distract you from nurturing an ongoing conversation with me. The voice of the enemy and the easy entertainment of the television can deceive you into thinking that time with me will not be productive or enjoyable. So you must decide not to listen to that voice but instead tune your ear to my voice. I have so much I will share with you as you listen to my voice.

I hear you calling me, not to a to-do list, but to yourself. I want to fill my life with what will matter for eternity—relationship with you . . .

I Am Making You Holy in Every Way

May the God of peace make you holy in every way, and may your whole spirit and soul and body be kept blameless until our Lord Jesus Christ comes again. God will make this happen, for he who calls you is faithful.   1 Thessalonians 5:23-24

My grand plan has always been to make you holy, as I am holy. My grace does not nullify this requirement, and my forgiveness does not make holiness optional. I am at work in your life, and I will not quit until that great day when you will stand before Christ with nothing to hide.

You should know that I will not settle for sanctifying only the areas of your life you freely open to my penetrating gaze. I will continue to press and probe so that I might cleanse the hidden motives, the closeted collection of unresolved animosities, the destructive patterns that have become so much a part of you that you can't see them for what they are. I intend to work my way through every aspect of your character and personality, your habits and your desires, exposing the corruption and contamination and bringing fresh new life.

However you want to do it, Lord, please do it. Whatever you need to get rid of, I'm letting it go. I'm opening my spirit, soul, and body to you . . .

I Will Reward Your Sincere Seeking

It is impossible to please God without faith. Anyone who wants to come to him must believe that God exists and that he rewards those who sincerely seek him.   Hebrews 11:6

I am not impossible to please. In fact, I provide to you exactly what I require from you: faith. I have given you the faith to believe that I am real, and I am a rewarder. I am not merely an impersonal cosmic force but a personal, loving, gracious God to those who seek me.

I gave you the desire to go after me, and then I rewarded your pursuit of me. And what is the reward I have given to you? I have given grace and forgiveness. I have rewarded you with the righteousness of Christ in place of your failed attempts at being right with me. But the most prized reward I have given is myself—in closer relationship and clearer understanding. I have rewarded your seeking by allowing myself to be found.

Even though all my instincts tell me that I must work my way into your good graces, your Word makes it clear that what pleases you is faith. May my life be a living display case for how real and rewarding you are . . .

I Am Filling Up Your Emptiness

Christ . . . fills all things everywhere with himself.
Ephesians 1:23

I want to bless you today by filling you up with myself. I know there are lots of things that compete with my filling, and many of them are very good. But know that you can fill up your life with many good things and still miss the best thing.

So today, will you make room for me to fill you with myself—my thoughts, my priorities, my love, and my concerns? Will you tune out other voices so you can hear mine? Will you eliminate empty activity so you can enjoy interacting with me?

You don't have to be afraid of losing out when you let go of something you enjoy to make room for me. I only add to your life. I will never deplete you or disappoint you.

Fill me, Lord Jesus, not just with good things, but with the very best thing: you. Show me what needs to be discarded from my life so you can fill me with yourself . . .

I Am the Light That Leads to Life

Jesus spoke to the people once more and said, "I am the light of the world. If you follow me, you won't have to walk in darkness, because you will have the light that leads to life." John 8:12

Most people in this world are stumbling through life in the darkness, unable to see the way forward that leads to ongoing life and joy. But because you follow Christ, you do not have to walk in the danger of the darkness. He is shining the radiance of my glory on you. I am flooding your life with the light of my very presence.

My Word is a lamp that shows you where to walk and what to avoid as you make your way through life in this dark world. My light reveals what is true in contrast to what is false, what is real in contrast to what is a fraud. As you walk in my light, you can see what is truly beautiful to behold, what is truly worthy of your worship, what is truly life-giving to your soul. My light will not lead you into a dead end but into everlasting abundant life.

Lord, open the eyes of my heart to see the supreme greatness of your wisdom and power. Heal my stubborn blindness. Fill me with the all-pervading, all-exposing, all-purifying, all-pleasing light of your presence . . .

I Am the Fountain of Living Water

For my people have done two evil things: They have abandoned me—the fountain of living water. And they have dug for themselves cracked cisterns that can hold no water at all!
Jeremiah 2:13

You have a tendency to look for blessing in the wrong places. Here I am, a fountain of living water that will bring you constant refreshment and satisfaction as you drink deeply of me. Yet you foolishly turn away from me to splash around in muddy pools.

You think you will find refreshment in the approval of other people. You think you will find relief from your fear of failure in your accomplishments. You think you will find fulfillment in having a picture-perfect family. You think you will find security in your savings and satisfaction in getting the latest thing. Yet have you noticed that these pleasures leave you still thirsty, unsatisfied?

I want to bless you with abundant life that will satisfy you now and into eternity. Bring your needs and desires to me and let me bless you.

Wash over me, Living Water. Wash away the dirt left from my wanderings in this world . . .

I Have Made You an Heir of My Glory

Since we are his children, we are his heirs. In fact, together with Christ we are heirs of God's glory. Romans 8:17

I have determined who will inherit this world and all that is in it. I have promised everything to the Son as an inheritance. In the end, Jesus will have all things under his complete control and ownership—all natural resources, all governmental power, all human intelligence, and all the riches of the earth. Everything will be under his authority and command.

And while Jesus doesn't have to share this inheritance with anyone, he will. He will share all he inherits with all of those who have put their trust in him. Because you are united to Christ, with Christ you will inherit it all.

Someday you will leave this earth and let go of everyone you have loved and everything you have enjoyed. You will be left with only your eternal inheritance. But you will not be disappointed. It will be everything you have anticipated and more.

I have no right to demand anything of you, Lord God, yet you intend to give me everything! Your generosity is beyond my comprehension . . .

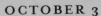

The Faith I Give You Is a Faith That Gets Busy

We are shown to be right with God by what we do, not by faith alone. . . . Just as the body is dead without breath, so also faith is dead without good works. James 2:24, 26

My grace that was given to you when you placed your faith in me is not idle or ineffective. It is busy in your life, producing good works.

You know this is true when, instead of hoarding more stuff for yourself, you find great joy in giving to those in need. You know your faith is alive when, instead of closing your eyes to someone who is hurting, you allow your heart to be broken. Your faith is shown to be living and real when you care for those who have nothing to offer you in return.

These good works are not what will save you—only the perfect goodness of Christ credited to you can save you. These good works are evidence that this saving transaction has taken place and you are now being sanctified by my grace.

Just as I breathe in the air around me and then breathe out, as I take in your goodness and kindness and love, may it flow out from me to the hurting world around me . . .

I Have Draped You in a Robe of Righteousness

I am overwhelmed with joy in the LORD my God! For he has dressed me with the clothing of salvation and draped me in a robe of righteousness.   Isaiah 61:10

Neither you nor anyone else can stand before me in your own stead, resting in your own goodness, boasting in your own worthiness. All attempts at righteousness apart from Christ are like filthy rags, which I cannot accept. So what will you do? How can you have any hope of being welcomed into my presence?

In fact, you will be gladly welcomed and accepted because I have orchestrated a great exchange. At the Cross, Jesus clothed himself in the soiled garment of your sin. When you turned to me in faith, I covered you in the pure and spotless robe of Christ's own justifying righteousness. And it is forever yours. No sin can strip you of that robe of righteousness. The day will come when you will stand before me and you will be pronounced righteous in the court of divine justice.

Like Adam, I had only fig leaves for covering my failure and shame. Like the Prodigal Son, I had only filthy rags and regret. But you have dressed me with the clothing of salvation and draped me in the robe of Christ's own righteousness . . .

I Will Replace Your False Idols

*Wherever we go we find people telling us about your faith in
God. . . . They keep talking about the wonderful welcome you
gave us and how you turned away from idols to serve the living
and true God.* 1 Thessalonians 1:8-9

False idols are cruel taskmasters. They demand sacrifice but
can never be satisfied. They promise to fill you up but only
deplete you in the end.

I want to identify and eliminate your false idols so that
you can experience the joy and freedom of worshiping me
exclusively. I will give you the grace you need for this painful
process through my penetrating Word, which I will use as a
spotlight and scalpel in your heart. My Spirit will aid in your
deliverance by helping you to identify your sin and pursue
a godly life. And I have surrounded you with brothers and
sisters in Christ who will teach you, lovingly confront you
about your idols, and provide encouragement and guidance in
your spiritual growth. The more rigorously you avail yourself
of these means of grace, the greater effect they will have in
delivering you from the idols that plague your soul.

*I know that the only way to squeeze the idols out of my heart,
leaving no room for them to return, is to make all-consuming
worship of you alone my top priority . . .*

I Give Myself to Those Who Will Receive Me

He came to his own people, and even they rejected him. But to all who believed him and accepted him, he gave the right to become children of God.   John 1:11-12

I am holding out the gift of Jesus to you. But it is up to you to receive that gift and unwrap it, making Jesus a part of your daily life rather than stashing him away on the shelf for when you might decide that you need him. To accept Jesus is to believe he is as good as the Bible says he is and to make him a part of your thought life, your pleasure-seeking, and the foundation of your hope.

While you may have been encouraged again and again to give your life to Christ or to give him your heart, that is not what I'm inviting you to do. The gospel is not about what I'm asking you to give, but what I'm asking you to receive. To receive Christ is to recognize that he is the most beautiful, most desirable treasure in the universe and to open up your life to him, saying, "I receive you. I welcome you. Come into my life and make yourself at home."

I am opening up my life, inviting you, Jesus, to come in from the fringes and establish yourself in the center . . .

I Know What to Hate and What to Love

You love justice and hate evil.   Hebrews 1:9

I know that you love to worship me as a God of love. But I also know that it can feel uncomfortable to you to worship me as a God of wrath. But if I did not have wrath, and if I did not have anger, then I would not be God. I am perfect in love on the one hand, and equally perfect in hate, on the other hand. Just as totally and perfectly as I love, so totally and perfectly do I hate. I know exactly what to hate. I hate evil.

You don't have to be embarrassed or offended by my wrath. The reason you sometimes feel that way is that you still have a ways to go in grasping and valuing my holiness. Until you do, you won't see sin as being that big of a deal. But as you feed on my Word and abide in me, you'll begin to hate evil the way I do. You will also grow to love justice like I do. You will no longer be afraid to look squarely at my wrath because you will see clearly that it flows out of my perfect justice and my holiness.

I refuse to edit the aspects of your character that I struggle to make sense of. I love you for who you are, God—for your perfect love and perfect hate . . .

I Will Forgive Even the Good Things You've Done

We are all infected and impure with sin. When we display our righteous deeds, they are nothing but filthy rags. Like autumn leaves, we wither and fall, and our sins sweep us away like the wind. Isaiah 64:6

My grace is good enough, my pardon is generous enough to forgive you for all of the wrong you have done. But it is even bigger than that. I will forgive you for the good things you have done with wrong motives. I will forgive your self-righteous efforts to appear devoted to me with no dependence upon me.

Self-righteousness is that list you have inside your head of what you've done or who you are that makes you acceptable to me, and certainly better than the average person around you. I will come and cleanse you of your church attendance and service you were hoping other people would notice, your sacrificial generosity you were hoping would put me in your debt, your vocal stand for a moral cause you were hoping would cover your own failures. I will credit to you the perfect righteousness of my Son.

All of my efforts to be good apart from your power are in vain. Keep showing me when I lose sight of you and seek to impress other people. Only the righteousness of Christ can make me acceptable in your sight . . .

I Have Redefined Your Life

God . . . made us alive together with Christ . . . and raised us up with him and seated us with him in the heavenly places in Christ Jesus.   Ephesians 2:4-6, ESV

There was a time when your separation from me because of your sin made you what you were. But I have united you to Jesus Christ so that you have been transformed from what you were to what he is. Now everything that belongs to Christ belongs to you.

Why does this matter? Because these realities change everything about your life. No matter what you've been through and who you've been, there are now three events that define who you are. When you trusted in Christ, you died with Christ, you were raised from the dead with Christ, and you ascended with Christ and are seated with him in the heavenly places. His story has become the story of your life. His blessings have become your blessings. I have relocated your worth and destiny in Christ. Whatever else may happen to you, nothing can alter this deep connectedness.

You have given me the very best seat in heaven—right in the midst of your throne—not because of what I have done or who I am, but because of what Christ has done and who he is . . .

I Will Not Disappoint You

We can rejoice, too, when we run into problems and trials, for we know that they help us develop endurance. And endurance develops strength of character, and character strengthens our confident hope of salvation. And this hope will not lead to disappointment.   Romans 5:3-5

So many people have made promises to you and let you down. So many opportunities have held out promise to you and have left you disappointed. So it makes sense that you might wonder if I will ultimately disappoint you.

But I am wholly other. Every promise I have made, I will keep. Every longing channeled toward me, I will satisfy. Every sorrow entrusted to me, I will redeem. I will not disappoint you in the end. I'm not suggesting that you will never feel disappointment in this life, but I want to use your disappointment in the here and now to cause you to sink the anchor of your life deeper into the hope of heaven.

I can see that the disappointing things about my life in this world are working to increase my confidence in your ultimate salvation, which I know will not disappoint me . . .

I Am Worthy of Your Quiet Reflection

Study this Book of Instruction continually. Meditate on it day and night so you will be sure to obey everything written in it. Only then will you prosper and succeed in all you do.   Joshua 1:8

You wake up to the blare of the radio and have the television on in the background. A steady stream of noise from the world takes up space in your head and shapes your thoughts. And all the while, I want to bless you by filling your mind with myself. I want you to enjoy the pleasure of contemplating me—what I am like, what I have done, and what it means to be in relationship with me. I want you to talk to yourself about me, arguing with your incorrect assumptions about how I am at work in the world and reasoning through your understandings of my Word.

It takes intentional effort to make mental space for quiet reflection. So make space for meditating on me. And when things get quiet, don't look for something to fill the silence. Let your soul go on a vacation from the noise of the world. Give your mind a break from the radio, the newspaper, and even great books, to think great thoughts about me informed by my Word.

Spending time in purposeful contemplation of you is not an obligation or duty you impose but a pleasure you invite me to indulge in . . .

I Will Empower You with Inner Strength

I pray that from his glorious, unlimited resources he will empower you with inner strength through his Spirit. Ephesians 3:16

My best work is done from the inside out. I am doing a glorious work on the interior of your life, in the place where your ambitions and opinions and intentions take shape. But while I am working on the inside, this work will not remain hidden deep inside you. What I am doing will become obvious to everyone around you as it works its way out in your behavior.

People will begin to notice that you are not so quick to look out for yourself first. They'll notice that the old cynicism is giving way to trust. They'll find that kindness and encouragement are replacing your old habit of dishing out criticism.

You do not have to come up with the resources to generate this kind of strength on your own. It is not up to you to work up the will to empower this kind of transformation. It is my unlimited resources that the Spirit will draw upon to bring about this refreshing change. He will make an invisible Christ visible in your life.

You've brought me so far, Lord, from who I used to be, but I have so far to go . . .

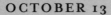

I Am Providing You with Security in the Shaking

All of creation will be shaken and removed, so that only unshakable things will remain. . . . We are receiving a Kingdom that is unshakable. Hebrews 12:27-28

When I laid down my law in the form of the Ten Commandments, the force of it shook the earth. And when I poured out my wrath on my own Son at the Cross, once again the earth shook. A day is coming when once again the earth will be shaken by the power of my judgment. But you need not fear. Your life is secure; your future is unshakable because your life is hidden in Christ.

It is not up to you to be strong or to have great faith as you face the future. What is important is that your life is built on a firm foundation—Christ alone. What matters is that my Word is at work in you, undergirding you. Security cannot be found in a job, in an insurance policy, in abundant health or wealth. All of these things are vulnerable to being shaken. But you, my child, are blessed with absolute security in the shaking.

I am receiving from you a Kingdom that is not vulnerable even to your wrath, that will one day shake the earth. I am safe and secure not because I am good, but because Christ is good and my life is hidden in him . . .

I Will Remember My Covenant

God said, "I am giving you a sign of my covenant with you and with all living creatures, for all generations to come. . . . When I see the rainbow in the clouds, I will remember the eternal covenant between God and every living creature on earth."
Genesis 9:12, 16

I have set a sign of my commitment to you in the sky. When you see a rainbow painted in its many colors, let it remind you of my mercy toward my own.

But you must know that the rainbow is not primarily a sign for you but for me. It reminds me of how I have bound myself to you. You will do well to remember my covenant and embrace it from the heart. However, your safety does not hang on your ability to remember but on mine. Your salvation is secured by divine power. Your looking to Jesus will bring you joy and peace, but it is my looking to Jesus that secures your salvation.

I see your gracious commitment to show mercy written across the sky in radiant color, and it reminds me that you have made eternal promises that you will surely keep . . .

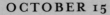

I Have Secured for You All That I Require of You

Therefore, my beloved, as you have always obeyed, so now, not only as in my presence but much more in my absence, work out your own salvation with fear and trembling.
Philippians 2:12, ESV

When I instruct you to work out your own salvation, I'm not telling you to go out and get what you don't have—more patience, more strength, more joy, more love. Your growth comes not as you work harder to get something you don't have, but as you live in the reality of what you have already been given—as you daily rediscover what I've already provided for you in Christ. This is the hard work you are called to.

As you focus less on what you need to do for me and more on all that I have done for you through Christ, you'll find my Spirit spilling out of your life in beautiful new ways. Your relationship with me is based not on your performance, but on Christ's performance credited to you. So you will grow, not by behaving better, but by believing better—believing in bigger, deeper, and bolder ways what Christ has already secured for you.

Because of the finished work of Christ, I already have the approval, acceptance, righteousness, and rescue I long for . . .

I Am Producing Fruit in Your Life

The Holy Spirit produces this kind of fruit in our lives: love, joy, peace, patience, kindness, goodness, faithfulness, gentleness, and self-control.   Galatians 5:22-23

Apart from the transforming work of my Spirit, you will naturally gravitate toward sexual immorality, impurity, jealousy, anger, and envy. But because you have been born of God, while you might be tempted toward these things, they will not define the pattern of your life. Instead, flowing out of your life will be evidence that my Spirit is at work, generating abundant fruit.

I will bless you with love for the unlovable people in your world, joy in the midst of great sorrow, peace in the midst of chaotic circumstances, patience for frustrating situations, kind words in place of a cold shoulder. You will do good to those who have nothing to offer you, be faithful when you want to quit, be gentle when you are treated harshly, and be self-controlled when you want to give in to temptation.

Holy Spirit, only you can generate this kind of fruit in my life. Make yourself at home and do your sanctifying work . . .

I Know You

I knew you before I formed you in your mother's womb.
Jeremiah 1:5

The greatest blessing in your life is knowing me—except, perhaps, for the blessing of my knowing you. You could never know me if I did not choose to know you. I am the One who initiates the relationship. I have no intention of relating to you as a nameless, faceless number. Even before you were born, I knew you and loved you personally. I know your greatest fears, your deepest hurts, and your most cherished dreams.

So the good news is that I know you. And the difficult news is that I really do know you. I know every thought, every feeling, and every experience. In fact, I know you better than you know yourself. I know your false intentions and mixed motivations that you may not be consciously aware of. I know your jealous thoughts and petty animosities. I know the worst about you, and I choose to love you anyway. No revelation of some secret sin can stop me from loving you or change my intentions to bless you.

I don't have to hide anything from you (as if I could!). You know me deeper than I know myself, yet you love me more than I can comprehend . . .

I Have Chosen You to Produce Lasting Fruit

You didn't choose me. I chose you. I appointed you to go and produce lasting fruit, so that the Father will give you whatever you ask for, using my name.   John 15:16

I have laid claim on your life. And it is my honor, not yours, that is at stake in the work I've called you to. My purpose in choosing you is not merely to forgive your sins and deliver you one day to heaven, but to make your life fruitful and productive.

I chose you to bear the fruit of genuine love for other people. The love you receive from Christ as you abide in him will flow through you and onto others for their benefit, so that they will turn to me and become my disciples.

I chose you to prevail in prayer and have the privilege of seeing heaven opened up to you. Your destiny is to be astonished forever at the outpouring of my goodness in answer to your prayers.

God, you have chosen me to pray in your name for more fruitfulness, and you have promised that you will give it. So I am asking . . .

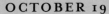

I Have Given You a Place to Start

Fear of the LORD is the foundation of true knowledge, but fools despise wisdom and discipline. Proverbs 1:7

Everyone needs a place to start in this life, a foundation for moving forward. And I have not left you on your own to figure out how to make life work. I have given you clear instruction on where to start if you want to live a life full of my blessing. You must begin with a healthy fear of me. Your fear of the Lord must guide the shape of your hopes and dreams.

Certainly the fear of the Lord is not the spirit of your times. Self-esteem is what people think is most needed. And while I have created you as a person of great worth, your own worth is not the foundation to build your life on. The fear of the Lord is the only sure foundation. Christ comes first. He is your most urgent need and the key to your future. As you start sensing the difference between self-esteem and Christ-esteem, you'll know that the idol of Self is losing its grip, giving way to the fear of the Lord.

Lord, I want true knowledge and wisdom, not the world's counterfeit. So I'm opening my life to your discipline. Chasten me. Correct me. Show me where I'm wrong. Teach me what is right . . .

I Reward Those Who Trust Me

You love him even though you have never seen him. Though you do not see him now, you trust him; and you rejoice with a glorious, inexpressible joy. The reward for trusting him will be the salvation of your souls.   1 Peter 1:8-9

It takes great faith to look squarely at hardship and suffering and say with confidence, "I can have joy because I know God is working in this situation to purify me." And this is just the kind of faith I am giving to you. I am at work to develop in you a deeper love for Christ, more confidence in my purposes, and an inexpressible, unexplainable joy in the midst of difficult circumstances.

Some people can see only what is in front of them—the suffering of this life. They have no eyes of faith to see me. But even though you cannot see me with your physical eyes, you have seen me revealed in my Word. You have staked your life and your future on my promises. And you will not be disappointed. You can rest in knowing that though you have not yet seen me with your eyes, one day you will. And you will be eternally glad.

I am trusting you, Lord. And I don't believe I'll be disappointed. I believe everything you have promised will be even better than I've imagined . . .

I Have Given You Something to Consider

Think of all the hostility he endured from sinful people; then you won't become weary and give up.   Hebrews 12:3

When you feel sorry for yourself because your life is hard . . . consider Christ. Consider the difficulty of his life of poverty and opposition, and don't lose heart. When you feel forgotten by those who you thought cared about you . . . consider Christ. Consider what it was like for him to be rejected and ridiculed by his own family. Consider what it was like in those moments on the cross when even I turned away and he felt forsaken. Consider him and don't give up.

When you feel tired and you want to give up . . . consider Christ. Consider how he prayed into the night, his sweat falling like great drops of blood, only to endure trials and torture the next day after a night of no sleep. Consider him and you won't become weary. When you feel fearful about the future . . . consider Christ, who for the joy set before him endured the Cross, and think of the joy he wants to share with you.

Whenever I am tempted to give up and give in to disappointment or despair, I look to the Cross. I see the price you paid there so that you might call me your very own, and I keep going . . .

I Will Make Your Concerns My Concerns

Don't worry about anything; instead, pray about everything.
Philippians 4:6

Worry is a futile, frustrating, debilitating attempt to bear the burdens of life—and especially of the future—on your own, apart from me. But you are not apart from me, and so I'm calling you to turn your worries into prayers.

I'm not offering a magic formula or inviting a bedtime ritual of empty words. I'm calling you to the serious business of bringing your life before me and placing it under my care. Because while anxiety is an attempt to carry the burden of the present and future by yourself, prayer is yielding it to me and leaving it in my hands.

A life of prayer will cultivate a childlike trust. As your capacity to trust expands, your tolerance for uncertainty and ambiguity will grow and your anxiety will diminish. And you will experience peace—not numbness or unconcern, not the absence of inner or outward struggle, but my pervasive peace.

I'm entrusting my life, my concerns, my fears into your loving hands, Lord . . .

I Have Given You Armor to Resist Your Enemy

Therefore, put on every piece of God's armor so you will be able to resist the enemy in the time of evil. Then after the battle you will still be standing firm.   Ephesians 6:13

You have an enemy who is always scheming new ways to rob you of the joy of your life in me. But you are not left alone to protect yourself from his attack. I have provided everything you need to fight the spiritual battles in your life. You need only employ this spiritual armor.

The belt of truth pulls together all the spiritual loose ends in your life, calming confusion and correcting error. The body armor of righteousness is the increasing reality of holy living that makes you less vulnerable to flaming arrows of temptation. Shoes of peace enable you to walk as one who is no longer my enemy but has become my friend because of what Christ has done. The shield of faith deflects the enemy's lies, which try to convince you that the world will satisfy you more than I can. Biblical truths about salvation are your helmet, preserving your confidence and protecting you from doubt and discouragement.

I am strong in you, Lord, and in your mighty power. In your gospel you have given me everything I need to stand strong . . .

I Sent My Son to Save You, Not to Judge You

God sent his Son into the world not to judge the world, but to save the world through him. There is no judgment against anyone who believes in him. But anyone who does not believe in him has already been judged for not believing in God's one and only Son. John 3:17-18

The world sees me as an unbending judge, a God who takes pleasure in punishment. But you know better. You know that I am a righteous Judge, patient in exercising my judgment, generous in granting mercy and pardon. You know this because you have seen and embraced my Son. You have turned to him rather than away from him. You have believed in him, knowing that the judgment you deserve fell on him so that I can pour out my goodness and mercy on you.

So walk today in the freedom of one who does not fear judgment, in the joy of one who looks to the future and sees a glorious salvation.

Your judgment is no longer hanging over me, marking me for punishment. May my heart sing with joy that I have received salvation and need not fear judgment . . .

You Are My Masterpiece!

We are God's masterpiece. He has created us anew in Christ Jesus, so we can do the good things he planned for us long ago.
Ephesians 2:10

Your life is a product of my handiwork. You are who you are because of my doing, because of my grace at work in your life.

I've re-created you with a grand purpose in mind, and nothing can keep that divine decree from being accomplished—not your old nature that wars against you, and not the spiritual weakness that plagues you. Despite your daily battles with temptation and the ongoing opposition of the enemy, the outcome of your union with Christ will be holiness. This holiness not only perseveres but also advances.

My plans for your life are not just to make you beautiful but to make you useful. I want to bless your life by using you to bless the world around you with the grace and truth of Jesus.

I want to walk in the paths you've set out for me, Lord. Keep working in me so that I will not miss out on anything beautiful you have planned to do through me . . .

I Am Filling You with the Fruit of Your Salvation

May you always be filled with the fruit of your salvation—
the righteous character produced in your life by Jesus Christ—
for this will bring much glory and praise to God.
Philippians 1:11

The evidence that our relationship is genuine is abundant fruitfulness, which can come only from my work in your life. I have given you new resources to love the unlovable, a fresh spark of joy even in the midst of sorrow, a pervasive peace even when your circumstances are chaotic, an unexplainable patience in the face of frustration, and a heart that is kind instead of cold. I've given you a love for what is good instead of a fascination with what is evil, an unwavering faithfulness when it would be easier to quit, a compassionate gentleness when it would be easier to close your eyes to need, and an uncompromising self-control when it would be easier to give in to temptation.

This kind of character cannot be produced by human effort; it comes only as my Spirit works in your heart.

What a relief to know that I am not on my own as I try to
become all you want me to be. You are at work in my life,
producing the righteousness you desire . . .

I Am Calling You to Fix Your Gaze on Me

I lift my eyes to you,
*   O God, enthroned in heaven.*
We keep looking to the LORD our God for his mercy,
*   just as servants keep their eyes on their master,*
*   as a slave girl watches her mistress for the slightest signal.*
Psalm 123:1-2

Plenty of concerns clamor for your attention in this world.
But I am calling you to direct your heart's attention to me—
not just for occasional contemplation but for ongoing communion. As you find yourself daydreaming of lesser things,
turn your thoughts to me. When you find yourself wanting to
fill up the silence with the noise of the world, engage your soul
in conversation with me. What begins as an intentional act
of your will to set your heart and mind on me will become a
habit of soul, a spiritual reflex that brings you into the authentic closeness with me that you long for.

Fixing your inward gaze on me will free you from being
obsessed with yourself. And as you lift your eyes to me, you
will find friendly eyes gazing back toward you.

I long to set my inward gaze upon you, Lord, knowing that the
day is coming when I will see you in all of your splendor face-
to-face . . .

I Have Put My Glory on Display for You

The heavens proclaim the glory of God. The skies display his craftsmanship. Day after day they continue to speak; night after night they make him known.   Psalm 19:1-2

Look up, loved one! Can you hear what I'm saying to you in the skies above, and see what I've written for you in the wonder of creation? I am telling you about my greatness and goodness. I'm speaking to you of my presence and my creative power. I'm calling out to you to worship me.

Though this revelation is wordless and inaudible, the world around you is speaking to you of my existence, my glory, my identity and artistry as Creator. It is undeniable and unavoidable.

Though I am invisible to you, the universe I have made for you is a grand theater to showcase me and my works, a mirror in which you can contemplate my character and greatness. So look up, look around, and take in the wonder of my glory!

You have revealed yourself in the world around me, and I cannot ignore it. Fixed deep within me is an awareness of you and a sense of accountability to you . . .

I Will Be Your Sure Foundation in the Storm

Anyone who listens to my teaching and follows it is wise, like a person who builds a house on solid rock. Though the rain comes in torrents and the floodwaters rise and the winds beat against that house, it won't collapse because it is built on bedrock.
Matthew 7:24-25

You are discovering why I have given you my Word and called you not just to read it, but to think it through, dig deeply into it, and work it into your life. As you put my Word into practice, it is building for you a solid foundation that will enable you to withstand the storms of life.

Because you have really listened to what I am saying in my Word and have let it shape your thoughts, your values, your priorities, and your day-to-day conduct, you'll find that while storms still blow into your life, you won't be destroyed by them. Your world may be rocked by difficulty and disappointment, but your faith will hold firm.

Even when the clouds of difficulty and disappointment begin to gather over my life, I'm finding that I no longer cower in fear. Your Word has made me durable in the storms of life . . .

You Can Bring Me Much Glory

May you always be filled with the fruit of your salvation—the righteous character produced in your life by Jesus Christ—for this will bring much glory and praise to God.   Philippians 1:11

You were made and are being remade to bring glory to me. By this I don't mean that you can add to my glory. I mean that when people see in you that I matter in a wonderful way, I am glorified.

My glory is a weighty thing. It's not a burden, not something that weighs down your heart; in fact, the weight of my glory makes believers lighthearted. When you feel the weight of my glory, you will not feel the weight of lesser things. Disappointments and regrets won't matter so much because you have me, and I am all that matters to your happiness.

You glorify me when your heart is not weighed down with lesser things but is captured by one defining passion—to make my glory known in this God-trivializing world.

Lord, may my life be a billboard declaring your glory and goodness in this dark, distracted world that is not even looking for you . . .

I Have Taken Away Your Dread of Death

Yes, by God's grace, Jesus tasted death for everyone. Hebrews 2:9

When I invite you to look upon the death of Christ, I'm asking you to see it as more than a beautiful, inspiring example of dying for a cause; I'm asking you to accept that he has died in your place. That Jesus has tasted death as your substitute is the astonishing truth of the gospel, and one you can grasp only through faith.

Jesus drank the cup of my wrath for every cruel word you have spoken, every spiteful reaction, every selfish grab, every sexual indiscretion, every prideful attitude. And because he drank this cup as your substitute, you do not have to drink it. Because he tasted death, you will savor life.

Because Jesus experienced the judgment, the pain, the separation, the unknowns of death in your place, you don't have to be afraid of physical death. It will be your passageway into the eternal life in my presence that I've prepared for you.

It seems too good to be true that you have tasted death so I don't have to. I don't have to live with an inner turmoil and dread of death. Instead, I can look forward to unending life . . .

304 | OCTOBER 31

I Will Finish My Work within You

*I am certain that God, who began the good work within you,
will continue his work until it is finally finished on the day
when Christ Jesus returns.* Philippians 1:6

I took the initiative to draw you to myself and make you
new. Do you think it is now up to you to take it from here?
Of course not. You have not been left to yourself and to your
own resources to become more conformed to my image. Just
as I began my work in you by making you a new creation,
I am continuing my work in you, taking that which belongs
to Christ and making it increasingly yours day by day.

Because I made you and know you intimately, I know what
needs to be done. I have rolled up my sleeves and gone to work
at the core of your being—retraining your thought patterns
and reshaping your preferences as you feed on my Word. I am
knitting together your emotional wounds and taking down
your relational walls.

Trust in my methods and my timing. I am at work making
you fit for my heaven.

*Lord, give me confidence in you and patience with myself in
this process. I open up my life to you and invite you to do your
work . . .*

I Want to Save You from Superficiality

Let the message about Christ, in all its richness, fill your lives.
Teach and counsel each other with all the wisdom he gives. Sing
psalms and hymns and spiritual songs to God with thankful
hearts. Colossians 3:16

There is so much coming at you—hundreds of channels on
the television, Internet, e-mail, cell phones—so much calling
out for your attention. Enormous pressures hurry you from
one surface encounter to the next.

But I don't want you to settle for such a lightweight life.
My Word will be your salvation from superficiality. This will
happen not only as you read my Word in the privacy of your
home, but as you share and discuss it with others throughout
your day. My Word will move from being an assigned reading
to being part of the conversation. As my gospel is interwoven
into your thoughts and ideas as daily discourse, the wealth of
my wisdom will counteract the banality of this world's abundance of words.

Save me, Lord, from the triviality and superficiality of the
constant stream of this world's noise. Let me hear your voice;
let me speak your words; put your song in my mouth and I
will sing . . .

I Will Not Treat You as Your Sins Deserve

He will not constantly accuse us,
nor remain angry forever.
He does not punish us for all our sins;
he does not deal harshly with us, as we deserve.
Psalm 103:9-10

When hard things happen, many people cry out to me, "Lord, I don't deserve this!" or "Lord, this isn't fair!" You may think you want fairness from me, but you don't. Fairness would demand that I treat you as your sins deserve. And what you deserve is to be cut off from me, alienated from me for all eternity.

But my dealings with you are not grounded in fairness but in mercy. My unfailing love toward those who fear me is as great as the height of the heavens above the earth—so much more than you could ever deserve or merit. I have not done what is "fair" as the world defines fairness, yet it is perfectly just. I poured out my anger on my own Son so you can know my kindness. I dealt harshly with him, which he did not deserve, so I can love you in ways you don't deserve.

Forgive me, Lord, for ever thinking I deserve better from you.
Thank you for laying on Christ the punishment I deserve . . .

I Am a Savior Who Can Sympathize

Since he himself has gone through suffering and testing, he is able to help us when we are being tested.   Hebrews 2:18

There may be many things in this day ahead that will test you. Harsh words will test your patient rest in me. Physical pain will test your resolve to hope in me. Difficult circumstances will test your steadfast trust in me. But when you are tempted to despair or self-pity, resentment, anger, or unbelief, Christ will come to help you. He will come as One who knows, from his own agonizing experience, just what you are experiencing. And he will give you what you need to endure to the end.

Christ is able to help you when you are tempted because he has been tempted too. When you feel tempted to do what is easy rather than what is right, Jesus comes as One who was also tempted in that way. When you feel overwhelmed with demands on your time and energy, Jesus sympathizes. When you feel crushed by the sorrows of this broken world, Jesus understands.

You are not a God who has remained distant from the hard parts of living in this world. You entered my reality so I can go to you not only for salvation but for sympathy . . .

My Word in You Teaches You to Pray

If you remain in me and my words remain in you, you may ask for anything you want, and it will be granted! John 15:7

Plenty of people look for a formula to get what they want from me. But I want to show you how to pray so that your wants actually come from me. It is as my words abide in you—as the words of your Bible become so much a part of you that they begin to shape your prayers—that your voice will become one with mine in prayer. This is how you can ask whatever you want and it will be done for you. As you saturate yourself in my Word, I will purify your wants and magnify my will.

As you pray the Bible back to me, you will be lifted out of your own boring pettiness into the grandeur of my thoughts and the delights of my will. Praying for my will to be accomplished in your life is not a way of resigning yourself to something small. This is how I save you from your own smallness.

Now I see that so many of my prayers are too small for your massive blessing to fit inside. Only as my desires are shaped by your Word do they become big enough for you to satisfy . . .

I Have Cleared Your Record of Wrong

Oh, what joy for those whose disobedience is forgiven, whose sin is put out of sight! Yes, what joy for those whose record the LORD has cleared of guilt, whose lives are lived in complete honesty!   Psalm 32:1-2

You can be one of the happiest people in the whole world because you know that you are a sinner who does not deserve to be forgiven, and yet you've been forgiven. The sin that left such an ugly mark on your conscience and crippled you for so long has been washed away and put out of sight.

You don't have to live trying to cover up your past failures. You don't have to hide from me, from other people, or even from yourself. You can live out in the open—not because you are perfect and never sin, but because you know your sin will not be held against you.

The devil would have people think that to be really happy you need to escape my rules and live for your own selfish pleasure. But you know better. You're discovering the outrageous joy of living life as a forgiven sinner set free.

What a relief to come clean before you and live clean before you, Lord. I am well aware of my guilt and disobedience, but because of your grace, they will not have the last word in my life . . .

Your Life Flows from Mine

The LORD God formed the man from the dust of the ground. He breathed the breath of life into the man's nostrils, and the man became a living person.   Genesis 2:7

My child, you are like nothing else in all of my creation. Though I made you from the most lowly matter possible—dust from the ground—I have infused you with the most significant and glorious of substances—my very own breath! Though you are made of dust, you are far more than dust. You are also spirit because I breathed my own life into you. So even as you fill your lungs with breath in this moment, let it be a reminder of my love for you and the blessing I have given to you through my life-giving kiss.

I was spiritually dead until you came and breathed new life into me, Holy Spirit. Fill me with the life that flows only from you. May the very air I breathe remind me of your life-giving love.

I Have Handed You the Cup of Salvation

I will lift up the cup of salvation and praise the LORD's name for saving me. Psalm 116:13

Imagine a cup filled with the white-hot, punishing anger I have against sin. Imagine that my fury against everything evil has been distilled into liquid form and poured into a cup. Then imagine being asked to drink this dreadful drink. This is what Jesus faced as he prepared to go to the Cross. This was a cup he did not want to drink, praying three times for me to take it away if that were possible. Jesus agonized as he anticipated the anguish of drinking the cup of my judgment and experiencing the resulting break in relationship with me.

But he did drink it—every last drop—so that you will not have to. He drank it so that you will never have to experience my judgment or a break in your relationship with me. Because he drank the cup of my wrath, you have been handed another cup, not filled with judgment but with salvation. This cup of salvation will never be emptied but is always full and overflowing.

I deserve to drink from the bitter cup of wrath, but Christ has emptied that cup in my stead. You have handed to me the cup of salvation. I will drink deeply from it with great gratitude . . .

I Have Taken Away Your Self-Loathing

John saw Jesus coming toward him and said, "Look! The Lamb of God who takes away the sin of the world!" John 1:29

You have looked and seen my Lamb, who has taken away the sin of the world. Yet sometimes your bent to continue punishing yourself shows me that you wonder if his sacrifice was enough to erase your record of wrong.

The blood of the Lamb of God has satisfied me on your behalf. Rather than demand your blood, I've provided my own. Christ's sacrifice was big enough for the world and therefore big enough for you. And if my conscience is satisfied, shouldn't yours be?

This is my grand goodness to you in Christ: I do not throw your sin in your face; I take it all away. The blood of Jesus has removed everything you wish weren't true about you. All of your guilt, failure, shame, and regret have been cleared away so that they no longer factor into my attitude toward you. And it is all my doing, not yours at all.

I reject my condemning emotions in regard to my failures as well as my prideful entitlement in regard to my moral victories. Instead, I set my heart on the Lamb who has taken my sin away . . .

I Will Lift You out of the Pit

I waited patiently for the LORD to help me, and he turned to me and heard my cry. He lifted me out of the pit of despair, out of the mud and the mire. He set my feet on solid ground and steadied me as I walked along. Psalm 40:1-2

Sometimes this life drags you down into the pit of despair. When you've reached your breaking point, when you've run out of patience, when expectations have exceeded your energy, when the attack is imminent, cry out to me. Your prayer doesn't have to be pretty or well conceived; it will be beautiful to me. I love to answer the childlike prayers of my children. But you must be willing to wait. When my help seems long in coming, continue to wait rather than run ahead. Refuse to impose a deadline on me. Let me be God to you by submitting to my timing. Wait for me in humility and hope, knowing that at the right time, in the appropriate way, I will act.

I will lift you out of your hopelessness, moving you from the desperation of the pit to the security of a rock. And when I do, you will sing. All of the old songs will be new.

Now I can see you have a purpose in the pit. You are using the dark places in my life to generate a renewed appetite for you . . .

I Have Given You Something to Boast About

Those who wish to boast should boast in this alone: that they truly know me and understand that I am the LORD who demonstrates unfailing love and who brings justice and righteousness to the earth. Jeremiah 9:24

I love to hear you boast—not in a prideful exuberance about your own accomplishments or your impressive intelligence, power, or wealth, but in humble celebration of who I am, what I've done, and what I will do.

Many people in this world love to hear themselves talk about their own ideas, their own accomplishments, their own opinions. All of that prideful talk only reveals their lack of true wisdom. There is only one kind of boasting that is worthy of many words: the truth that I, the One True God, have given you a mind to know me when you could not comprehend me on your own. Boast all day long about my passionate loyalty to you, which you know you do not deserve. Celebrate day by day your confidence that I will do what is right.

You are the Lord who demonstrates unfailing love and brings justice and righteousness to the earth and in my life. And I love you . . .

My Gospel Is at Work

I am not ashamed of this Good News about Christ. It is the power of God at work, saving everyone who believes—the Jew first and also the Gentile. This Good News tells us how God makes us right in his sight. This is accomplished from start to finish by faith.   Romans 1:16-17

This is the gospel: that Jesus Christ, the Righteous One, died for your sins and rose again, eternally triumphant over all his enemies, so that there is now no condemnation for those who believe but only everlasting joy. When you heard this gospel and believed, its power began to work in your life. And you will never outgrow your need for it. Savor its ongoing power day by day to save you and sanctify you. It is the only truth in all the world that will not let you down when you give your life to it in faith. It will bring you all the way through temptation, persecution, and death into eternal safety and ever-increasing joy in the presence of a holy and glorious God.

I welcome your gospel to do its ongoing work in my life. Let it melt my heart, renew my mind, and bend my will . . .

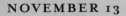

I Will Keep You from Stumbling

*Now all glory to God, who is able to keep you from falling away
and will bring you with great joy into his glorious presence
without a single fault.* Jude 1:24

I know that you know what it is to stumble. "Little" sins trip
you up, and sometimes you fall flat on your face in enormous
failure. Does this mean you are disqualified from the race of
faith? Do you wonder if your wandering will take you away
from me forever?

Because you are in Christ, you are as likely to stumble and
fall away as he is—and you know that is impossible. Perhaps it
would be possible for you to go completely off course if it were
up to you to get yourself across the finish line of faith. But it
is not your personal prowess or internal will that will keep you
from stumbling. Christ will bring you into my glorious presence—faultless before me. He will present you before me not
as you are but as he is. When you stand before me, I will not
see your great failures but his all-surpassing sufficiency. That
day will not be a solemn occasion but a grand celebration!

*My Champion, if I'm on my own in this walk of faith, I will
never make it home. So protect me from that which would
cause me to stumble and fall. Hold me by the hand and bring
me home . . .*

I Will Wipe Away All Your Tears

He will swallow up death forever!
* The Sovereign LORD will wipe away all tears.*
He will remove forever all insults and mockery
* against his land and people.*
* The LORD has spoken!*   Isaiah 25:8

As tears well up from deep inside you, evidencing the broken-ness of your heart, look up to me and embrace by faith what is to come. The day is coming when I will wipe away all of your tears.

When you read about that day, about my plans to set all things right in this world, don't think that it will be an imper-sonal ending to the sorrow this broken world has brought into your life. You will know it is I who have taken away everything that has caused you pain. It will be my touch that will bring healing to all of the hurts in your life, my voice that will whisper words of eternal comfort, my embrace that will let you know that your loneliness is no more.

Sovereign Lord, only you can deal completely and eternally with the pain of living in this broken world. I'm longing and looking for your hand to one day wipe away all my tears for good . . .

I Will Not Condemn You

There is no condemnation for those who belong to Christ Jesus.
Romans 8:1

Here is the heart of my gospel, the essence of my goodness toward you: Though you are guilty of great sin, you will not be condemned to eternal punishment for it. Though I am the very one against whom you have sinned, I will plead your case and execute justice *for* you, not against you.

It is not that I do not condemn sin. It is that I condemned Christ for your sin so that there is now no condemnation for you. He absorbed the full measure of my wrath in your place. Because of this great act of substitution, no one can make a condemning charge stick against you. I have declared you righteous so that you can be confident of the final verdict of the last judgment: justified, not condemned.

I am always and forever for you in Christ Jesus and will never be against you. So live as one who has been set free from condemnation.

Jesus, I know that there is no condemnation for me only because you endured it in my stead. From your reservoir may I draw up buckets of mercy to extend to those around me . . .

I Have Given You a Great Treasure

I want them to have complete confidence that they understand God's mysterious plan, which is Christ himself. In him lie hidden all the treasures of wisdom and knowledge.
Colossians 2:2-3

Today I want to bless you with great wisdom and knowledge. This means that I want to show you what is worthwhile in this life and how you can become a part of it. I want you to know what is right and best so you can embrace it with everything you've got. There are lots of smart people in the world who point you in all kinds of directions to get ahead. But instead of looking around to discover what you need to know to make your way in this world, look to me. The more you explore the mystery of who I am and what I'm doing, the more you will discover the hidden treasure of the wisdom that comes only from me.

I want to know the mystery of God, which is Jesus Christ. I believe that I will find in you everything valuable and beautiful. Reveal to me this mysterious and glorious truth . . .

I'm Inviting You to Come to Me

Come to me, all of you who are weary and carry heavy burdens, and I will give you rest.   Matthew 11:28

You have heard Christ's invitation to come and have responded to it; you have come to him for salvation. But accepting this invitation to come is not something you do one time. It is something you must continue to do day by day. Will you continue to come to Christ with all of the burdens you carry that are so heavy and make you so tired—the burdens of painful memories, broken relationships, guilt, and grief? Will you come to Christ with the burden of trying to serve me without the power that comes from being constantly connected to me? Will you let Christ carry the heavy burden of being good enough for me? Christ has taken that weight from you. He carries the burden of all of your failed efforts to be good enough, and he gives you in return his very own perfect goodness.

I know that what you need most is real rest—not just for your body or from your schedule, but rest for your soul. Only Christ can give you soul-rest.

I hear your invitation to come. But I'm realizing that I run to so many other things to find rest and so many other people to share my burdens. So I'm coming to you, Lord . . .

I Have Given You Something to Focus On

Let us strip off every weight that slows us down, especially the sin that so easily trips us up. And let us run with endurance the race God has set before us. We do this by keeping our eyes on Jesus.
Hebrews 12:1-2

As you fall more deeply in love with me, you hate your sin more and more. But you are in for a lifelong battle against sin. Your struggle isn't something that you will be able to hurry through, no matter how determined you may be. Your change into the image of my Son is not like a sprint but an endurance race. Your sins are weights that cling closely to you, and it will take some time to strip them away.

You do not have to run from seminar to seminar, pile up self-help books, or spend your paycheck on psychotherapy to run this race. Instead of focusing on yourself and your closely clinging sin, you must focus on Jesus. Look away from the sin that is either alluring or condemning, and look to your Savior. Patiently focus all of your attention on him. Think on him. Ponder his ways. Consider his goodness. Rivet your thoughts on what he has done and what he will do.

I am fixing my gaze on you, Jesus, and finding it easier to say no to sin and yes to you . . .

I Have Adopted You As My Own Child

You have not received a spirit that makes you fearful slaves. Instead, you received God's Spirit when he adopted you as his own children. Now we call him, "Abba, Father."
Romans 8:15

There are two ways of relating to me. First, you can relate to me as a slave, seeing me as a God who barks orders and threatens punishments, driving you along with a whip. While this slavish fear may appear to produce good behavior on the surface, it will not foster a real love relationship.

Instead, I want you to relate to me as my own beloved child, chosen and adopted into my family. The Spirit of adoption has bent down and kissed your guilty heart with my love, taking away the grim, hard heart of a slave and arousing in you a glad tenderness toward me as your Father. As your confidence in my love for you increases, you'll know that you can tell me anything and I will still love you and heal you.

Papa, you have taken me in and made me your own through the finished work of Christ. Your Spirit is changing my deepest feelings about you so that I can feel safe under your protective love . . .

I Will Teach You to Be Content

I have learned the secret of living in every situation, whether it is with a full stomach or empty, with plenty or little. For I can do everything through Christ, who gives me strength. Philippians 4:12-13

I want you to learn something—something that will make what seems unbearable bearable, something that will turn inconveniences into opportunities to experience Christ in newer and deeper ways. I want to teach you to be content.

Perhaps you think you'll be content when you finally get what you want, but real contentment is being willing to accept less than or something other than what you want. Christ himself is your source for the spiritual strength you need in order to live with what you didn't ask for and with less than you want. So when you have an unmet need, an unfulfilled desire, an unresolved injustice, or an unrelieved pain, see that I am inviting you into the classroom of contentment. I want to bless you by teaching you to find your contentment in Christ alone. He will supply from himself whatever you lack in the here and now.

Rather than focusing on the misery of my situation, I am at peace as I focus instead on the sufficiency of my Savior . . .

I Will Heal What is Hidden

The word of God is alive and powerful. It is sharper than the sharpest two-edged sword, cutting between soul and spirit, between joint and marrow. It exposes our innermost thoughts and desires. Nothing in all creation is hidden from God. Everything is naked and exposed before his eyes, and he is the one to whom we are accountable.   Hebrews 4:12-13

I know that your instinct, especially when you know you've done wrong, is to hide from me. You forget that I do not condemn you but instead want to cleanse and heal. And nothing can be hidden from me anyway. I know your secret thoughts and your hidden agendas. So instead of hiding from me, open my Word and hear from me.

Don't stand over my Word as its judge. Open your life underneath my Word and let it judge you. As you read and meditate, it will go to work on you like a surgeon's scalpel, cutting away the evil that has invaded the interior of your life. Let its demands engage with your will and move you to glad surrender. Let its wisdom reorder your priorities and reshape your perspective. Let its promises become the source of your hope. When you invite me into the hidden places of your heart, you will not suffer shame but will find healing.

Shame tells me I must hide the ugly parts of my life and character from you. But yours is not the voice of shame, but of power to change . . .

I Will Make You Overflow with Thankfulness

Let your roots grow down into him, and let your lives be built on him. Then your faith will grow strong in the truth you were taught, and you will overflow with thankfulness.
Colossians 2:7

Many harmful attitudes would like to penetrate the walls of your heart and mind—like greed, self-centeredness, and a sense of entitlement. Once inside, these thought patterns wreak havoc on your relationships and steal your joy. But if you want to keep them out, there is a guard that will protect you. That guard is gratitude—chosen intentionally in the words you speak and the attitudes you nurture. Ongoing gratitude is like a guard against sinful attitudes that attack, making themselves at home.

Shallow whining simply can't find a foothold in the heart of a grateful person. There's no room for demanding behavior in the life of a grateful person. The same lips that offer thanksgiving are less likely to complain or blame or gossip. Giving voice to gratitude leaves little room for prideful boasting. So let this thankfulness overflow in your life, and find yourself at rest in my provision.

As my roots go deeper into you, my sense of entitlement is being put to death and genuine gratitude is growing in its place . . .

I Have Given You an Anchor for Your Soul

We who have fled to him for refuge can have great confidence as we hold to the hope that lies before us. This hope is a strong and trustworthy anchor for our souls.   Hebrews 6:18-19

When the winds of difficulty blow in your life, you are not at their mercy. I have given you an anchor that holds you secure. While you will not be unaffected by the storms that blow, you will not be destroyed by them.

So reach out and grasp the hope I am holding out to you. Don't reach for lesser salvations or risky securities in the storm. Tether yourself to something solid. Take hold of the hope I have held out to you in Jesus Christ. The hope I offer is not unbridled optimism despite evident realities. It is not escapist denial. It is centered in the reality that Jesus is everything you need for this life and the next.

You do not have to live this life with your fingers crossed, always looking for the positive outcome. You can live at peace, with your heart and life securely anchored in my promises and protection.

I am tethering myself to you, Lord, confident that you will see me through the storms of this life and safely into the next . . .

Pleasing Me Promises Benefits Now and Forever

Physical training is good, but training for godliness is much better, promising benefits in this life and in the life to come.
1 Timothy 4:8

The Christian life is not merely a set of doctrines to be accepted but a power to be experienced. The mark of truly belonging to me is that my power flows into your life, making you more and more pleasing to me. And while I provide the power, godliness is something you must dedicate yourself to. Growth in godliness requires your devoted effort and must be fought for. And while the fight is not going to be easy, it will be easier if you train yourself for it.

As you discipline yourself through prayer, meditation, and feeding on my Word, you'll find that you have the grace you need when the challenge comes. When someone is unkind, you'll be able to overlook it because you've been in my presence and basked in my kindness. When you're tempted toward lust, you'll be able to look the other way because you've been fixing your gaze on my beauty. You've been training yourself so that you can respond in godliness when the challenge comes.

As I discipline myself for godliness, you are giving me a heart that longs to please you . . .

I Infuse Your Work with Significance

*Work willingly at whatever you do, as though you were working
for the Lord rather than for people. Remember that the Lord
will give you an inheritance as your reward, and that the
Master you are serving is Christ.*   Colossians 3:23-24

Whatever you do for a living is the business of heaven, and
therefore worthy of your enthusiasm. This means your pri-
mary motivation to work is not simply to earn money and
buy things, but to honor me and benefit others. It means that
your boss is not your boss; Christ is. Your company does not
provide for you; Christ does. It means your success is not the
result of personal achievement, but a gift of my grace.

Whatever you do today—whether you're doing the dishes,
running a corporation, selling products, or serving food—
you can do it all for my glory. I infuse the whole landscape
of human experience with my glory, making every legitimate
human employment a holy calling. If you belong to me, your
job is not just a job; it's a calling. It is my grace entering into
your experience and thereby giving it significance.

*I know that any success I experience is not self-made. You
have provided everything I need so that my work has become
worship . . .*

I Am for You

What then shall we say to these things? If God is for us, who can be against us? Romans 8:31, ESV

There is much in this world that is against you. People turn against you, circumstances go against you, your own appetites and affections work against you. But none of that ultimately matters because of who is for you: I am for you. Hear it again and let it go down deep: I am for you and will never turn against you.

This means that I, the Lord of the universe, the Maker of heaven and earth, the Holy One, the Almighty, Abba, the All-Sufficient One—I am on your side in the daily struggle. To have me as your friend is to have everything, whatever else you may lack. Not to have me is to have nothing, whatever else you may own.

Am I against your sin? Yes. If I were indifferent to it, I wouldn't be on your side. But because I am for you, I have accepted the sacrifice of Christ on your behalf so that sin is no longer a barrier between us. I can be all-out for you.

If I did not have Christ I would be on my own, with no God in heaven who is for me. But I am not on my own. You are really for me . . .

I Will Not Let Your Life Be Ruled by Luck

We can make our plans, but the LORD determines our steps. . . .
We may throw the dice, but the LORD determines how they fall.
Proverbs 16:9, 33

Because you belong to me, nothing happens in your life as a result of mere luck, fate, fortune, destiny, or chance. You are not at the mercy of such things. Instead, I am involved in what may appear to be fate or coincidence to bring about my plans and purposes. I am at work behind seeming good luck to bring you success, and behind seeming bad luck to teach you to trust me.

Every step you take, every word you speak, everywhere you go, and everything you think and feel—it is all under my direction. I am ruler over all of the events of history so that they work together for good for those who love me. Because you know I am in control of your life, you can refuse to see yourself as a victim of bad luck. You can embrace humility in the best of circumstances, knowing that I am working behind the scenes to bring about the outcome I desire.

What a relief it is to me to know that my life is not ruled by fate or luck but by your sovereign loving hand. I gladly invite you to have your way in my life . . .

I Am Developing Discernment in You

Solid food is for those who are mature, who through training have the skill to recognize the difference between right and wrong. Hebrews 5:14

In the Ten Commandments I have given you a list of dos and don'ts that show you how to live. You don't have to wonder if it is okay to steal money from someone's wallet, steal the affections of someone's spouse, or covet someone else's position or possessions. But when it comes to deciding what television programs to watch or avoid, whether to drink alcohol or abstain, whether to invest in a company with questionable practices or invest that money in another way, you need discernment. You can't depend on your natural instincts. At least you can't when you first come to me. But as you mature—as your mind is renewed, your desires are retrained, and your values and priorities are replaced—you will find that I am reshaping your natural instincts.

Discernment develops as you nourish yourself with my Word. It will become a part of you and teach you how to distinguish good from evil. What used to be acceptable to you will become so distasteful that you won't want it anymore.

As your Word goes deeper in my life, so many of my choices are becoming clearer . . .

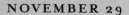
I Want to Move You from Duty to Delight

*Jesus replied, "The most important commandment is this:
'Listen, O Israel! The LORD our God is the one and only LORD.
And you must love the LORD your God with all your heart,
all your soul, all your mind, and all your strength.'"*
Mark 12:29-30

Doing your duty toward me is not an altogether bad thing.
But I know that duty will only get you so far. If our relationship is only about duty, it will drain you and leave you dry.
Duty is not enough to keep you clinging to me when the bottom falls out. The coldness of duty chills the warm and loving
relationship I want to have with you.

　Your sense of duty is an insult to my love and will leave you
cold. What I want is your passionate delight in me, which will
bring you joy. Duty shows up for worship with its hands full,
wanting to give to me. But delight shows up for worship with
hands empty, wanting to be filled by me. Duty expects to be
recognized and rewarded for personal sacrifice. But delight
knows that the sacrifices of God are a broken spirit and a
broken and contrite heart.

*All of this doing my duty has only filled me with self-
righteousness and taken me away from you. Take away my dry
sense of duty and fill me with delight in you . . .*

I Have Delivered You from the Fear of Dying

Only by dying could he break the power of the devil, who had the power of death. Only in this way could he set free all who have lived their lives as slaves to the fear of dying.
Hebrews 2:14-15

Death is terrifying for people who have no hope beyond what they've been able to collect or accomplish in this life, or for those who have no confidence that facing me in death will be sweet. Fear rules them like a silent master in the form of denial, distraction, or drivenness.

But death is not terrifying for you. You know that the only weapon the devil can use to make your death miserable is your sin. But your sin has been forgiven and paid for in the death of my Son, so the devil has no power to destroy you in death. And I have everything in my hands to bless you in death.

While you will likely experience physical death unless Christ returns first, you need not dread your dying. My Son absorbed the damning agonies of death so that you need not fear.

If your anger is gone and your grace is working for my good, then I can stare death in the face without denial and without fear . . .

I Replace Good Things with the Best Thing

Fix your thoughts on what is true, and honorable, and right, and pure, and lovely, and admirable. Think about things that are excellent and worthy of praise. Philippians 4:8

Your life is filled with so many good things. You are busy earning a living, exercising your body, caring for your family, serving the church, caring for your neighbors. These are good things.

But I also know how good things can crowd out the best thing—unhurried, unhindered, intimate time and energy invested in listening to me speak to you through my Word and pouring out your heart to me in prayer. So many distractions suggest to you that other activities are more productive, more interesting, more urgent. But refuse to be distracted away from me.

The abundant life I intend for you is not a life busy with good things but a life fixed on the best thing. Jesus is true. Jesus is right. Jesus is pure. Jesus is lovely. Won't you admire him?

There is so much noise in my life that threatens to distract me from hearing your voice and fixing my thoughts on you. Keep wooing me to you, Lord . . .

I Will Keep You from Perishing

For God loved the world so much that he gave his one and only Son, so that everyone who believes in him will not perish but have eternal life. John 3:16

I want to lead you into a settled assurance in my love. But you must look for it where I have placed it. I've given you a gorgeous creation to live in, a body that heals, a mind that can figure things out, and relationships that make life rich. But all of these earthly gifts come and go. If you base your confidence in my love for you on your health, your safety, or any of my other gifts that are tied to this world, you will never be sure of me. This is why I have revealed my love with clarity and finality, by giving you what is most precious to me—my Son. I have given my Son to you so that you will not perish. This is love.

While I created mankind to live forever, the reality is that you are very perishable. But I do not want you to perish. I want you to live forever before me with life in all its richness and fullness. And because you entered into my saving love when you believed in my Son, you will not perish. You will live.

Your love is great enough to wrap its arms around the whole world, and good enough to wrap around me so that I will not perish; I will live . . .

I Am Freeing You from the Tyranny of Things

*God blesses those who are poor and realize their need for him,
for the Kingdom of Heaven is theirs.*   Matthew 5:3

Within the human heart there is a stubborn root of the self-
life that seeks to possess and possess some more, coveting
things with a deep and fierce passion. And your heart is no
different, evidenced by your regular use of the words *my* and
mine. Sin has made the good gifts I have given you a potential
source of ruin to your soul. An abundance of possessions that
demand to be protected and improved upon threaten to take
the place in your life reserved solely for me.

I want you to live in the fullness of my blessing. Allow me
to root from your life the possessions that have set themselves
up as a rival for your affection and attention. I intend to free
you from the tyranny of always wanting more and from the
rigor of holding on to what you have with such a fierce grip.
While you may appear to lack many things, you will know
deep in your soul that in fact you possess everything—because
everything that belongs to me belongs to you.

*Root from my heart all of those things I have cherished so long
that they have become a part of me. When they are gone, enter
my heart and dwell there without a rival . . .*

I Will Give You the Very Best Gifts

Keep on asking, and you will receive what you ask for. Keep on seeking, and you will find. Keep on knocking, and the door will be opened to you. . . . If you sinful people know how to give good gifts to your children, how much more will your heavenly Father give the Holy Spirit to those who ask him. Luke 11:9, 13

When you read in my Word that you are to "keep on asking," you might think that the secret formula for getting what you want from me is to wear me down by repeating your request. Or you might think that the purpose of asking others to pray for you is that if enough people are praying, I will relent to give you what you're asking for.

But while I value and invite your perseverance in prayer, don't continue to pound on the door of heaven repeating your same request while refusing to listen to me. Come in and talk to me. Share your heart with me, and let me share mine with you through my Word. Asking, seeking, and knocking have little to do with getting what you want from me, and everything to do with enjoying more of me in your life by my Spirit.

I'm coming to you again, Lord, asking for the very thing I know you want to give me—your Holy Spirit, your very best gift . . .

I Am Worth Pondering

All who heard the shepherds' story were astonished, but Mary kept all these things in her heart and thought about them often.
Luke 2:18-19

At this time of year, many people around you will give plenty of thought to purchasing presents, planning travel, and preparing for programs and parties. But few will truly give themselves over to pondering the import of my becoming flesh and entering into the world. This season and throughout the year, will you make time to ponder the significance of my coming?

Ponder my glory and the angel's announcement. Ponder the work of my Spirit and the wonder of God being born of a woman. Feel the joy of the shepherds and fall before me in worship like the wise men. Consider my faithfulness in fulfilling my promise to Abraham and connect the dots with my promises still to be fulfilled. Marvel at the humble coming of this One who made the world and will save the world. Honor me and enrich yourself by thinking through everything about the glorious mystery of God becoming man.

Lord, I choose to ponder all that your Word tells about your coming. Give me eyes to see the wonder of it, and a heart that overflows with the joy of it . . .

I Reveal Myself in Ordinary People and Places

You, O Bethlehem Ephrathah, are only a small village among all the people of Judah. Yet a ruler of Israel will come from you, one whose origins are from the distant past. Micah 5:2

When I sent my Son to be born in a small and unimpressive village called Bethlehem, I turned every expectation upside down. Jesus came as a baby instead of a grown man. He was born to ordinary parents, not people of prominence or power. He came as a humble teacher rather than a conquering king. And he was born in an obscure little town rather than in one of the great cities of his day.

This should tell you something about how I choose whom and what I will use and bless. I don't choose on the basis of accomplishment, reputation, or worldly value. I choose to use simple, ordinary things and people so that I am the One who gets all the glory. You do not have to be impressive or powerful to garner my loving attention. I am the One who brings all of the significance to our relationship. You will find your significance in having my presence in your life.

I am grateful to know that you came to ordinary people in an ordinary place, because I am ordinary and I long for you to come to me . . .

I Always Act at Just the Right Time

When the right time came, God sent his Son, born of a woman.
Galatians 4:4

Though it is hard to wait on me, and though it may some-times seem to you that I am slow, my timing is always perfect.
I am never late. I always act at just the right time.

I knew when the time was just right to send Jesus, the Messiah, into the world. I knew when the exact religious, cul-tural, and political conditions were in place. You see, I am not making up plans as I go. All the grand events of my plan for your redemption have been scheduled in advance, from Creation to the enslavement and exodus of my people from Egypt, to David taking the throne in Israel, to the birth and death of Jesus, to the day when Jesus will return.

The course and timing of history is not a mystery to me. Time is in my hands. And I will bring about my plans and purposes in the world and in your life right on time.

You are the God of history, and time is in your hands. I know that you can be trusted to accomplish everything you intend in the world and in my life in your perfect timing . . .

DECEMBER 8

The Son Given to You Gave Himself for You

For a child is born to us, a son is given to us. . . . And he will be called: Wonderful Counselor, Mighty God, Everlasting Father, Prince of Peace.   Isaiah 9:6

The names given by the prophet Isaiah show how Christ reveals himself to you because you believed. As the Wonderful Counselor, he has the best ideas and strategies; he's the wisest and most perfect teacher. If you listen to him, you'll know what to do. Because he is the Mighty God, you can be confident that he will use his power on your behalf, helping you to overcome sin and the attacks of the enemy. As the Everlasting Father, you can rest in his loving care, certain that his affection has no limits. As the Prince of Peace, he has invited you into his Kingdom of full and perfect happiness, giving you the assurance of safety and security. He is on his throne enriching his people with every blessing.

The baby who was born to you became your strong deliverer and your source of security and satisfaction forever. The Son whom I gave to you gave himself for you.

Wonderful Counselor, guide me. Mighty God, rule over me. Everlasting Father, take care of me. Prince of Peace, give me your peace . . .

I Made Myself Touchable and Knowable

We saw him with our own eyes and touched him with our own hands. He is the Word of life. This one who is life itself was revealed to us, and we have seen him.   1 John 1:1-2

What I've called you to and provided for you is not merely a philosophy to embrace, a creed to follow, or a moral code to live by. I'm not primarily interested in getting you to follow my program or promote my agenda. There is no life-giving power in simply imparting an unattainable standard.

I want you to see me and embrace me as a person, not merely as a program. That's why I became touchable, knowable, vulnerable. I came to you in the most easy-to-receive way I could—as one of you—so that I could breathe life back into you.

This life I brought to you is not just a message to agree to, and not a secret that only a favored few are privy to. I have put the life you long for on open display in Jesus.

While I have not seen you with my own eyes or touched you with my own hands, I have the reliable record written by those who did, and I believe . . .

I Made My Home among You As One of You

The Word became human and made his home among us.
John 1:14

You could never have made your way to me on your own; I had to come to you. The Word by whom the world was made and is governed contracted himself into a virgin's womb. He took upon himself the whole nature of a human being, fully and totally identifying with all that it means to be human.

Jesus became human so that his life would be intertwined with those he came to redeem—and so that humanity could see me up close. The eternal Word utterly identified with humanity in every way, feeling the hurts you feel, experiencing the limitations you face. But it was more than that: he became mortal. Only flesh can die; a spirit cannot die. If Jesus, the eternal Son of God, had remained forever with me in glory in heaven, he could not have died. This is the grace planned from eternity past and executed in time and space—that I came to you in the person of Jesus, and made my home among you, so that I could make you mine.

You came, Jesus, to make your home among us—to show us what God is like, and to give yourself in our place. Please make yourself at home in my life . . .

My Grace Transforms Even the Hard Things

Gabriel appeared to her and said, "Greetings, favored woman! The Lord is with you!" Confused and disturbed, Mary tried to think what the angel could mean. "Don't be afraid, Mary," the angel told her, "for you have found favor with God!"
Luke 1:28-30

You need never fear when you know that I am the One at work in your circumstances. You have found favor with me, which means that my grace is actively at work in your life—even in the things that are perplexing, disturbing, and bring you pain, the things that do not fit into your plans.

When you belong to me, you can be sure that whatever I allow into your life I will use for good. In my hands, these things become gifts of my grace toward you as I use them to shape you and make you into a person I can use in this world for my grand purposes.

It takes faith to see the hard things in your life as gifts of my grace—faith to rest in who I am and the love I have for you. When you have that kind of faith, you can be confident I am doing something good in and through even your difficult circumstances.

God, give me faith to entrust myself to you even in the hard places of life. Fill me with faith to trust you with whatever you ask of me . . .

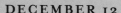
You're Blessed Because You Believe in My Word

Elizabeth gave a glad cry and exclaimed to Mary, "God has blessed you above all women, and your child is blessed. . . . You are blessed because you believed that the Lord would do what he said."   Luke 1:42, 45

Many people in this world do all kinds of things seeking to earn my blessing. But my blessing is not something that can be earned or manipulated out of me apart from simple belief in me. If you believe that the eternal God became a human person in Jesus Christ, and if you take that firm confidence into the center of your life, you're blessed, transformed, utterly changed. To be blessed is to be brought back to full shalom, full human functioning. I bless you by making you everything I meant for you to be, strengthened and repaired in every one of your human capacities.

Christ was willing to go through the whole of human experience, from the trivial irritations of family life, the cramping restrictions of hard work, to the horrors of pain and humiliation, defeat, despair, and death. And it was all so that I could bless you—a blessing you receive by believing.

I believe that you did what you promised in sending your Son, and that belief has put me in a place of abundant blessing. It pours over me and into me, and I love you for it . . .

I Am Worthy of Magnificent Praise

My soul magnifies the Lord, and my spirit rejoices in God my Savior. Luke 1:46-47, ESV

While you can never fully take in my actual greatness, you can magnify me from your soul. You magnify me not by making me bigger or more beautiful than I truly am, but by making me greater in your thoughts, in your affections, in your memory, and in your expectations. You magnify me by having higher, larger, and truer thoughts of me. You magnify me by praising me and telling others about my greatness so that I will be exalted throughout the earth.

Sometimes you wonder why you aren't happy, why you make sinful choices, why you feel distant from me. Often it's because you have small thoughts about me and magnified thoughts of yourself—your wants, your rights, your accomplishments. But what you need most is not for me to make much of you. What will bring you deep satisfaction is to make much of me.

Lord, deep in my soul I choose to magnify you today. I want to magnify you in my conversations and in my heart. Forgive me for my small thoughts of you. May you be magnified! . . .

I Always Keep My Promises

He has helped his servant Israel
  and remembered to be merciful.
For he made this promise to our ancestors,
  to Abraham and his children forever.   Luke 1:54-55

The children of Israel were greatly blessed in Old Testament times as they held on to my promise. Mary recognized that in the baby she carried I was fulfilling the promise I made to Abraham to bless the whole world through one of his descendants. In this child were the promised mercies, the abundant forgiveness, the true knowledge of me—every blessing I have always intended to give.

As you gaze into the wonder of the fulfillment of my promise to send a Savior, enjoy the blessing of increased confidence in everything I have promised you. I may not always fulfill my promises in the way you want or in the timing you expect, but I will never fail to fulfill every promise I have made. I have promised I will never leave you or forsake you—and I will not. I have promised to work all things together for your good—and I will. I have promised to complete the work I began in you—and I am accomplishing that even now.

I'm staking my life and my future on the reliability of your promises, Lord . . .

I Am Strong Enough to Save You from Your Sin

An angel of the Lord appeared to him in a dream. "Joseph, son of David," the angel said, "do not be afraid to take Mary as your wife. For the child within her was conceived by the Holy Spirit. And she will have a son, and you are to name him Jesus, for he will save his people from their sins."   Matthew 1:20-21

What is that sin that seems to have a hold on your heart and mind today, the sin that keeps interrupting our fond fellowship? Whatever it is, I sent my Son to save you from it.

The name I gave for my Son was a name rich with meaning about who he would be and what he would do. It meant that this baby would be a rescuer, a savior. Jesus is "the Lord saves." I sent him to rescue you from the sin that would keep you apart from me for eternity—not only in a judicial sense, but also in a practical sense. His love overflowing in your life will rescue you from the sin of self-love. His power at work in your life will save you from your sinful impulses.

There is no one else and nothing else that can save you. Jesus is the God who saves, and you need to be saved!

I turn to you and believe that you are strong enough to save me from my sinful self . . .

I Will Clothe You in Humility

She gave birth to her first child, a son. She wrapped him snugly in strips of cloth and laid him in a manger.   Luke 2:7

From the day he was born, Jesus' clothing said something significant about who he is and what he is like. The way he dressed reflected the attitude of his heart—humble and lowly. Instead of holding on to his own uninterrupted glory, Jesus chose to leave behind the robes of glory that were his in heaven to be wrapped in rags. He became as much of an earthly servant as he had been a heavenly sovereign.

Later, on the night before he died, Jesus took off his robe, wrapped a towel around his waist, and began to wash the dusty feet of his disciples. This was servant's work, an act of deep humility and service. Throughout his life and as he faced death, Jesus showed you what it looks like to clothe yourself in humility—not in outer clothing but in the inner attitude of your heart.

This is the way I intend to clothe all those who are disciples of Jesus—in the clothing of a humble servant. I will make you more and more like my humble Son.

I want to be clothed in humility, to willingly and joyfully take the role of a servant in this world . . .

I Have Entered into Your Mess

She gave birth to her first child, a son. She wrapped him snugly in strips of cloth and laid him in a manger, because there was no lodging available for them.   Luke 2:7

There is no part of your life that is too dark or dirty for me to enter in. I am the God who condescends, who enters into the messiest, most shameful parts of your life to transform it into a place fit for the God of the universe to dwell. Just as the King of Glory was birthed into the filth of an animal stall, I will come into the places in your heart and life that are unpresentable, embarrassing, and have not been exposed to the light.

So throw open the doors of your heart and invite me in. I will not come to condemn or criticize but to cleanse and re-create. It does not matter what the past has been; I will forget and forgive. It is not worthiness I am looking for. All I ask for is your emptiness, your nothingness, your want of feeling and goodness and grace—all these will be but room for me.

Though I am unworthy and unclean, you have come to lodge within my heart. You are cleansing my heart and transforming it into your glorious throne . . .

I Give Humble People a Glimpse of My Glory

That night there were shepherds staying in the fields nearby, guarding their flocks of sheep. Suddenly, an angel of the Lord appeared among them, and the radiance of the Lord's glory surrounded them. Luke 2:8-9

When I broke my centuries-long silence to announce that the waiting for my Anointed One was over, it was not the social or religious elite I sought out. I do not bow to human culture's caste systems or conventions. I bend down to reveal the glories of my eternal plan to those who are quiet enough to hear me, and humble enough to recognize their need of me.

That night the shepherds saw the periphery of my presence, as I gave them a glimpse of my glory written across the sky. I made my glory visible, drawing aside the curtain of the heavens so they could see into ultimate reality—the glory of my being, which is always there but is hidden from full view. This is the glory you will one day share with me. On that day your humility before me will be rewarded with the great glory you will share with me.

Before your radiant glory I bow, and for your radiant glory I gladly wait . . .

My Glorious Light Shines on the Heart

*That night there were shepherds staying in the fields nearby. . . .
Suddenly, an angel of the Lord appeared among them, and the
radiance of the Lord's glory surrounded them.*   Luke 2:8-9

Everything I have ever made shows my glory in some way or
another. My glory is what brightness is to the sun, what wet is
to water. It is like the heat of a fire, the emanation, the product
of my presence, the revelation of myself.

But I have not limited the revelation of myself to the
impersonal manifestations of my glory in creation. I have
given you a greater disclosure, a fuller revelation. I have spoken clearly through my Word, disclosing my glory in a way
that communicates truth and gives instruction.

But the fullness of who I am has been revealed as never seen
before in Jesus Christ. He is the personal embodiment of the
brightness of my glory. Just as the radiance of the sun reaches
to the earth to provide light and warmth, so in Christ you
sense the warmth and radiance of my glorious light touching
your heart.

*As I fix my gaze on Christ, I not only see your glory, I am being
transformed into your glorious likeness. So I will fix my gaze on
you . . .*

I Bring You Good News of Great Joy

The angel reassured them. "Don't be afraid!" he said. "I bring you
good news that will bring great joy to all people. The Savior—yes,
the Messiah, the Lord—has been born today."   Luke 2:10-11

The guilty conscience responds in terror when I make myself
known. But I have broken through your terror to come to
you, not in judgment but in mercy, in the flesh-and-blood
presence of my Son. This is the good news the angels brought,
which should bring you great joy: I have done the greatest
thing I could do for you, which is to give you a Savior. Your
good intentions are simply not strong enough to control your
evil impulses. You need a Savior to rescue you from yourself.

Because you have seen your need for a Savior and have
come to Christ, you will not always be the way you are now.
Neither will the world always be the way it is now. The Savior
has come, and evil is doomed. Your best days are still ahead.

The gospel gives me a hope beyond everything that threatens
to beat me down in this world. And it gives me joy beyond the
temporary pleasures of this world. I receive this good news of a
Savior with joyful relief and reverent awe . . .

I Know What You Need Most

I bring you good news that will bring great joy to all people.
The Savior—yes, the Messiah, the Lord—has been born today
in Bethlehem, the city of David! Luke 2:10-11

The best gifts are those from someone who has taken the time
to get to know you well enough to discover what you enjoy
and what you need. My greatest gift to you reveals that I know
you intimately. I know what you will enjoy and what you need
most. My gift reveals that I know all about your glaring flaws
and desperate poverty. I know that as good as you may look
on the outside, there is something deeply wrong on the inside.

What you need most is a Savior. You need someone who
is good enough and strong enough and loving enough to save
you from your determination to save yourself. I have given
you Jesus, who came to take care of your most significant
problem—your separation from me because of sin.

Your great gift was not in giving Jesus as an example to show me
how to live, but in giving him as a substitute to die in my place.
As I celebrate his birth, I know that this salvation required his
death, and I am in awe of such a gift . . .

My Glory Is Higher Than the Height of Your Sin

Suddenly, the angel was joined by a vast host of others—the armies of heaven—praising God and saying, "Glory to God in highest heaven." Luke 2:13-14

My armies broke through the heavens—not to make war but to bring peace. That night I sent my Son—not to administer swift justice but to mediate reconciliation. My angels sang— not about your offense toward me but about my grace toward you. This is my great glory—my abundant grace toward sinners, offered through Jesus Christ.

The most relevant message to this sin-ruined world was, is, and always will be "Glory to God in highest heaven." The best news for sinners is that whatever you may have done or may do, I am still God. I reign over all and I will not allow evil to succeed in my world. My glory is supreme over all other realities. Hear the song of the angels celebrating that something is higher than the height of human sin—my divine glory.

How I long for the day when your glorious Kingdom is finally consummated. Then there will be perfect peace on earth for those with whom you are pleased because they are in Christ . . .

I Sent My Son to Make Peace

Glory to God in highest heaven, and peace on earth to those with whom God is pleased.   Luke 2:14

I did not send my Son to make war against my enemies but to make peace with them. Christ came to turn my enemies into friends.

Whether you realize it or not, at one point you were my enemy. Left on your own, you would never choose me; you would fight against me. But I have not left you on your own. Even though you declared war on me deep in your heart, I have declared peace on you. This friendship was made possible not through Jesus' birth but through his death.

Even though you've rebelled against me, I have reached out to you, making the first move toward you to make peace. I have given you the grace to overcome your natural resistance toward me so that we can develop a deep friendship. I have given you the faith to trust in me, making you one of those with whom I am pleased.

Thank you, Jesus, for coming to make peace rather than to make war. I know that it is only as I hide myself in you that I am pleasing to God. So I come to you and join myself to you by faith . . .

I Came to Serve You

Even the Son of Man came not to be served but to serve others and to give his life as a ransom for many.   Mark 10:45

I have not hung up a "Help Wanted" sign in the world and before you, but a sign that says "Help Available." Christ did not come to earth to recruit workers, but to do a great work. He didn't come because he had needs you could meet, but to meet your great need.

While I am pleased when your heart is inclined to serve me out of love, I want you to know that my greatest aim is not to be served by you but to serve you. I want you to place your faith in me—not in what you can do for me, but in what I have done for you through Christ. And then, out of your love for me and a desire to be like me, I want you to serve the world around you.

This life I've called you into is not about doing for me; it is about receiving from me. I am serving you by blessing you with acceptance, forgiveness, freedom, and joy. So let my goodness to you fill you up and spill out into the lives of others.

Your gospel is too good to be true and so much more than I deserve. It is changing my orientation toward you from a sense of duty to delight . . .

Christ Became Poor so You Could Be Made Rich

You know the generous grace of our Lord Jesus Christ. Though he was rich, yet for your sakes he became poor, so that by his poverty he could make you rich.   2 Corinthians 8:9

Long before he came to earth, everything belonged to the Son. The glory and joy, the power and privilege of heaven were all his. But to come to earth, he left it all behind. Jesus gave up the riches of heaven to become a poor person on earth. To become poor meant a laying aside of glory; a voluntary restraint of power; an acceptance of hardship, isolation, ill-treatment, malice, and misunderstanding; and finally death. He was born as a baby in a stable so that as a man he might hang on a cross.

Jesus gave up his close relationship with me when he took your sin upon himself at the Cross. In this way, he became poor so that you could become rich—not rich in regard to money, but rich in relationship with me. He became poor so that you can one day enjoy all the riches of heaven that he let go of when he came to earth.

Jesus, you did not come to earth to get something from me but to give me everything that has real and lasting value. You have made me truly rich . . .

I Have Given You My Very Best

He who did not spare his own Son, but gave him up for us all—how will he not also, along with him, graciously give us all things?   Romans 8:32, NIV

I am the most generous Giver in the universe, and for eternity you will be on the receiving end of my generosity. Yet everything I will give you, including heaven, is small compared to my greatest gift already given to you—Christ himself.

Because I have already given my own Son to you and for you, you can be confident that I will not fail to give you everything else I have promised, beyond all you can ask or imagine. I took everything away from my own Son so that I can give everything to you. I was harsh to my own Son in order to be sweet to you. I poured out my wrath on my own Son at the Cross so that I can pour out my grace on you. I sacrificed my own Son so that you will not have to sacrifice anything but will gain everything. In the sacrifice of my own Son I have made the greatest investment in you that I can think of.

How could I ever think of the Christian life as a sacrifice? I don't sacrifice anything! Instead, I stand to gain everything! Love so amazing, so divine, demands my soul, my life, my all . . .

I Have a Better Blessing for You

A woman in the crowd called out, "God bless your mother—the womb from which you came, and the breasts that nursed you!" Jesus replied, "But even more blessed are all who hear the word of God and put it into practice."   Luke 11:27-28

To be the mother of my Son was a great blessing I bestowed on Mary. But an even better blessing is available to you. Greater than the blessing of giving birth to Christ is to hear and obey my Word. It is a greater blessing to have Christ in the heart than in the womb.

To truly hear my Word is to be given spiritual understanding as my Spirit makes it known to your soul, and to receive it as true and real and certain. To be blessed is to respond to my Word not only by understanding it or being inspired by it but by consenting to its commands. It is to have your perspective and practice governed by my precepts.

Hearing and keeping my Word brings the happiness of a spiritual union and communion with me that far exceeds any kind of surface communication or connection.

Don't let me remain indifferent to your Word, Lord. As I hear your Word and put it into practice in my life, may Christ be formed in me . . .

I Provide the Power for Change

The message of the cross is foolish to those who are headed for destruction! But we who are being saved know it is the very power of God. 1 Corinthians 1:18

You know you need to change, but you feel powerless. Look to the Cross of Christ, and let my gospel work in your life to generate real and lasting change. It will give you the strength you need to withstand the pull of an addiction, the staying power you need to persevere in your marriage, and the endurance you need to bear an unbearable situation.

The same determination that kept Jesus walking toward the Cross is available to you as you persevere in obedience to me. The same strength that enabled Jesus to withstand ridicule is available to you as you encounter those who belittle your faith. The same ability to forgive that Jesus showed to those who nailed him to the cross is available to you as you seek to forgive those who hurt you. And the same force that brought Jesus back to life is available to rejuvenate the dead places in your heart where you think you cannot come alive to me.

The message of the Cross is power not only for my salvation but also for my transformation . . .

I Am Making Everything New!

*I saw a new heaven and a new earth, for the old heaven and
the old earth had disappeared. . . . And the one sitting on the
throne said, "Look, I am making everything new!"*
Revelation 21:1, 5

When you come to the end of the Bible, you might expect an
ending. But instead, you find a fresh beginning for literally
everything. You discover that I am in the process of transforming the world so that everything in it will be made new. When
you hear me say that I am making everything new, perhaps
you think I will replace what is old. But I am not making new
things; I am making everything new. This will not be just a
new coat of paint over something that is still old, but a complete remaking of everything so that all things will be new in
terms of quality, freshness, brightness, and strength.

This new heaven and new earth will include everything
over you, around you, and under you—everything you see
and hear and touch and experience. I do not intend to take
you away from this earth for eternity. Instead, I intend to
make this earth completely new—to make it a place where I
will live forever with you.

*You are not only going to resurrect my body, making it
completely new, you are going to renew your entire creation
and live with me in it . . .*

I Have Taken Away Your Fear of the Future

She is clothed with strength and dignity, and she laughs without fear of the future. Proverbs 31:25

Plenty of people wake up day after day with a heavy cloud of anxiety about the future. And I know that you, too, are sometimes tempted to fear—wondering whether your income will meet your expenses, if your relationship will recover from the turmoil, and if your plans will come to fruition or futility. But because you belong to me, you have no cause for fear as you prepare to enter into a new year.

You are clothed with strength and dignity. Your strength comes from resting and relying on Christ, and your dignity flows from your connectedness to King Jesus. The year ahead may hold new joys and opportunities, and it may hold new hardships and hurdles. But you can greet whatever comes, confident that I am your refuge and strength. You can laugh as you think about what may be ahead in the year to come—not because you are sure that you can handle it, but because you are sure that I can.

I want to see the new year as an adventure of trusting you in new ways and seeing your faithfulness in new forms. As I look forward, I will not fear; I will smile . . .

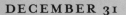

I Have Given You Something to Look Forward To

I focus on this one thing: Forgetting the past and looking forward to what lies ahead, I press on to reach the end of the race and receive the heavenly prize for which God, through Christ Jesus, is calling us.   Philippians 3:13-14

As I give you the new beginning that comes with a new year, I invite you to take stock. Are the things you're doing with the life I've given you helping or hindering you from making progress in what is most important—the one thing that will matter for eternity—your relationship with me? I want you to make progress in the life of faith so that you love and trust me more tomorrow than you did yesterday.

Today is a good day to look back, look forward, and look inward, viewing yourself as I see you and your life as I see it. But more important than looking inward is looking upward to Christ. Looking at Christ will give you a goal to pursue, a Person to enjoy, a passion to feed. Looking to Christ will orient the direction of the coming year—and of your entire life.

As I look into the coming year, I long for you to become the one thing that everything else in my life revolves around, the one thing that everything else in my life flows from . . .

SCRIPTURE INDEX